G. Maher

The Law of Inhibition and Adjudication

The Law of Inhibition and Adjudication

George Lidderdale Gretton, BA LLB WS, Solicitor
Lecturer in the Faculty of Law, University of Edinburgh

London/Edinburgh
Butterworths/The Law Society of Scotland
1987

United Kingdom	Butterworth & Co (Publishers) Ltd, 88 Kingsway, LONDON WC2B 6AB and 61A North Castle Street, EDINBURGH EH2 3LJ
Australia	Butterworths Pty Ltd, SYDNEY, MELBOURNE, BRISBANE, ADELAIDE, PERTH, CANBERRA and HOBART
Canada	Butterworths. A division of Reed Inc., TORONTO and VANCOUVER
New Zealand	Butterworths of New Zealand Ltd, WELLINGTON and AUCKLAND
Singapore	Butterworth & Co (Asia) Pte Ltd, SINGAPORE
South Africa	Butterworth Publishers (Pty) Ltd, DURBAN and PRETORIA
USA	Butterworths Legal Publishers, ST PAUL, Minnesota, SEATTLE, Washington, BOSTON, MASSACHUSETTS, AUSTIN, Texas and D & S publishers, CLEARWATER, Florida

British Library Cataloguing in Publication Data

Gretton, George Lidderdale
  The law of inhibition and adjudication.
  1. Executions (Law)——Scotland
  I. Title
344.1107'77   KDC898

ISBN 0 406 10433 6

Typeset by Latimer Trend & Company Ltd, Plymouth
Printed in Great Britain by Dotesios (Printers) Ltd
Bradford-on-Avon, Wiltshire

For M.W.G.

Let us now peruse our ancient authors, for out of the old fields must
come new corne—Coke (4 Co Inst 109)

Decreets would be of no effect, but as bees without stings, if the law
did not fix the kinds and form of the execution thereof—Stair (Inst
4,47,1)

Carmina vel coelo possunt deducere lunam—Virgil (Ecl VIII, 69)

Preface

I hope that this attempt at a restatement of the law of inhibition (with some account of adjudication) does not stand in need of an apology. The main text on the subject is still that of Graham Stewart (1898). Since the appearance of that great work not only has the law continued to develop but the frequency with which inhibition is used in practice has increased markedly. Whatever the deficiencies of the present work, the pressing need for modern treatment is not in doubt.

Inhibition cannot be discussed in isolation from its sister diligence of adjudication. But since the latter has in modern practice become uncommon, I have kept its treatment within the bounds of a single chapter. That of course does not do it justice. But it is hoped that even so short a treatment may be of use, especially nowadays when to many this diligence is a closed book. I would add however that there seem to be some signs of a revival in the use of this important type of process.

Apart from George Joseph Bell (whose treatment of inhibition in his *Commentaries* has been accorded by the courts a status that can only be described as quasi-statutory) and apart from Stewart, the literature on inhibition can be surveyed in very few words. There is a useful conspectus in Green's *Encyclopaedia*. Burns's *Conveyancing Practice* contains material, familiar to most conveyancers, on inhibition in relation to searches. The standard texts on Court of Session procedure give accounts of the creation and recall of inhibitions. (Here one must mention not only the treaties of Maclaren and Maxwell but also the work on Petition Procedure by McBryde and Dowie.) Inevitably, however, texts on conveyancing and on procedure are able to treat inhibition only from their own point of view. They cannot give a general account. Turning from inhibition to adjudication, there is again some account given in the standard texts on conveyancing and on procedure. Then of course there is the great work of Stewart. The only other source which requires mention is John Parker's little-known *Notes on the Diligence of Adjudication* (three editions, 1850, again 1850, and 1858).

Inhibitions and adjudications are of importance to the court practitioner, to the insolvency practitioner, and to the conveyancer. The present work seeks to meet the needs of all of these. In attempting to do this I have thought it right not merely to collect the relevant statutory material and the leading cases, but also to try to give guidance in the many situations which arise in practice but which are regulated by no clear authority. Sometimes this is possible by simple inference from settled principles. Where this is not possible I have tried to offer at least an informed opinion. Where later cases have appeared to me to be inconsistent with earlier and higher authority I have generally thought it right to follow the latter, attempting always to explain the nature of the difficulty.

I am very conscious that this work will be found to have faults both of commission and omission. For these I offer my apologies. I will be grateful to be put right by those more learned that myself. Correspondence will reach me at the University of Edinburgh, Faculty of Law, Old College, South Bridge, Edinburgh.

George Lidderdale Gretton
February 1987

Contents

Table of statutes and statutory instruments

Table of statutes

Table of cases

Abbreviations

Apart from the usual abbreviations, the following are used in this work:

1868 Act = Titles to Land Consolidation (Scotland) Act 1868
1924 Act = Conveyancing (Scotland) Act 1924
1970 Act = Conveyancing and Feudal Reform (Scotland) Act 1970
1979 Act = Land Registration (Scotland) Act 1979
1985 Act = Bankruptcy (Scotland) Act 1985
1986 Act = Insolvency Act 1986

Bell = G. J. Bell's *Commentaries* (7th edition, by McLaren, 1870)
Burns = John Burns, *Conveyancing Practice* (4th edition, by
    MacRitchie, 1957)
Stewart = J. Graham Stewart's *Diligence* (1898)

CHAPTER 1

Introduction

Scope of chapter

The first part of this chapter gives a brief summary of the law of inhibition and adjudication (inevitably involving an element of over-simplification). The second part of the chapter deals with certain other introductory matters.

Nature of inhibition

Inhibition is a diligence against the heritable (immoveable) property of the debtor. More specifically it strikes at such 'debts and deeds' voluntarily granted by the debtor after the date of the inhibition as affect or may affect his heritage to the prejudice of the inhibitor. Inhibition is a universal diligence in that it affects the totality of the debtor's heritable property in Scotland. The creditor need not specify, and may not even know, what heritable estate the debtor has. The effect of inhibition is to freeze the estate, thereby preventing the debtor from dealing with it, whether by sale or security or otherwise. A transaction which violates the inhibition is not void but is voidable at the instance of the inhibitor. Such a reduction benefits only the inhibitor. The transaction remains valid in a question with other parties.

Inhibition is a 'freeze' diligence, resulting in litigiosity, rather than a 'seize' diligence, resulting in nexus. It thus gives the inhibitor no real right in the debtor's heritage. If the debtor enters into fresh transactions with other parties after the date of the inhibition, the inhibitor will have a preference over such parties, but he can have no preference over parties whose rights existed already at the date of the inhibition. Thus if there are no post-inhibition transactions, the inhibition will be without effect.

Inhibition strikes only at the future voluntary acts of the debtor. Thus it does not prevent the debtor from completing transactions which he was already contractually bound to perform. Similarly, a sale by a heritable creditor would not be prevented by an inhibition against the debtor, provided that the heritable security pre-dated the inhibition.

As merely a freeze diligence, inhibition confers no right to possess the debtor's estate, or to sell it, or to participate in the free proceeds in the event of a sale by another party (such as a heritable creditor). To acquire such rights the inhibitor must use further diligence. (Though in practice of course inhibition on its own is often sufficient to bring about a voluntary settlement.) In theory this means he must adjudge the estate, though in practice this is not common. (But inhibition and adjudication are not two steps of one diligence. A creditor may adjudge without inhibiting.) Alternatively, if the estate has been turned into a liquid form as a result of a sale by another creditor, the inhibitor must arrest the free proceeds. Often however an inhibition is soon followed by the sequestration or liquidation of the debtor, rendering further diligence neither possible nor necessary. In such a case any preference created by the inhibition as against post-inhibition parties may be claimed directly through the bankruptcy process.

The effects of inhibition in barring the sale of, or the granting of security over, the estate, are referred to in this book as the first two effects of inhibition. There is also a third effect. This is that debts contracted by the debtor, after the date of the inhibition, even though not secured over the heritage, are postponed to the claims of the inhibitor in any process of realisation and distribution of the heritage. Debts contracted before the inhibition are unaffected.

Procedure in inhibition

Inhibition is solely a Court of Session process. Though it can be used on the dependence of, or in execution of, Sheriff Court actions, this can be done only by application to the Court of Session. This rule applies also to the recall of inhibitions.

Inhibition may be used (a) in execution of a decree or (b) on the dependence of an action or (c) on a document of debt. The last of these is not now common. Inhibition will be recalled if it is oppressive or if there is an appropriate tender of caution for or consignation of the sum sued for or such smaller sum as may be determined by the court.

Inhibition must be served on the debtor, and must be recorded in the Register of Inhibitions and Adjudications in Edinburgh. (This register is in practice usually called the Personal Register and is so referred to in this book.) It takes effect at the date of recording. But in certain cases it is competent to record a Notice of Inhibition before the inhibition itself. In that case the inhibition takes effect not from its own date but from the date of the Notice, provided that it is recorded not more than 21 days after the Notice.

Formerly the only method of obtaining inhibition was by bill and letters. The bill is an application for authority to inhibit. It narrates the decree or depending cause or document of debt, and other relevant circumstances, on which it is based. Once it has received the fiat (ie has been granted) it becomes authority for the letters to be signeted. The signeted letters are then served, and the inhibition is recorded in the Personal Register. This procedure by bill and letters remains competent and is often the only means possible. But in inhibitions on the dependence of a Court of Session action, warrant can be obtained as part of the summons, or, thereafter, by motion.

Inhibition may be recalled by petition in the Court of Session. But an inhibition on the dependence of a Court of Session action is normally recalled by motion.

Inhibition is extinguished (a) by payment (b) by voluntary discharge (c) by recall (d) by lapse (e) by the death of the debtor (f) by quinquennial prescription.

Relation to other procedures

In procedural matters, inhibition is closely linked with arrestment. There is something approaching identity as to grounds of use, warrants, recall and so forth—in general, the topics dealt with in chapters 2 and 3 of this book. In these matters an authority on arrestment will usually be an authority on inhibition also, and vice versa. Therefore, although in this text there is, in the interests of brevity, little cross-reference to arrestment, the reader should bear in mind that if there is no authority on a question involving inhibitions, it is worth while checking to see if there is authority on the corresponding point in the law of arrestment.

It must be stressed that this similarity is largely confined to procedural matters. As to substantive effect, there are radical differences between the two diligences, and apparent parallels are likely to mislead. For instance, whereas arrestment and furthcoming are two stages of a single diligence, so that there can be no furthcoming without a prior arrestment, inhibition and adjudication are two distinct diligences, so that it is perfectly competent to adjudge without first having inhibited. Again, whereas inhibition is only a freeze diligence ('litigiosity') arrestment is a seize diligence ('nexus'). (On the nature of arrestment, see Sim, 1984 SLT (News) 25.)

A procedure which has some similarity to inhibition is interdict against disposal. In some cases they are alternatives: thus in an action for divorce with financial conclusions it is competent for the pursuer to use either interdict or inhibition against the defender to prevent him from disposing of his estate. (See the Family Law (Scotland) Act 1985, ss 18 and 19.) Nonetheless, interdict against disposal and inhibition are very different in their nature. Interdict forbids disposal on pain of punishment. Inhibition imposes no such sanction. Conversely, in the event of breach of interdict the pursuer has no remedy against the property itself, whereas a disposal in breach of inhibition, unlike interdict, is a diligence against the heritable property of the debtor.

Obsolete forms of inhibition

As well as inhibition in its usual sense, there were formerly two other procedures which also bore the name of inhibition. They were inhibition of teinds, a process whereby the titular of teinds put an end to a tack of teinds, a process long obsolete, and spousal inhibition, whereby a husband could terminate his wife's praepositura, abolished by s 7(2) of the Law Reform (Husband and Wife) (Scotland) Act 1984. These two processes are mentioned only to be dismissed from further notice, since they are not part of existing law.

Quasi-inhibition

There exist certain types of notice, such as notice of litigiosity, which have an effect similar to inhibition. These are discussed in chapter 12.

Outline of adjudication

Unlike inhibition, adjudication is a seize diligence, giving the adjudger a judicial heritable security over the subjects adjudged. Again unlike inhibition, which affects the totality of the debtor's heritage, adjudication strikes only at such heritage as may be specified by the adjudger. A third crucial difference is that adjudication proceeds by way of special Court of Session action. Thus whereas a creditor who holds a decree for payment can proceed at once to inhibit, he cannot adjudge without raising a fresh action against his debtor.

Procedure is by way of Court of Session action. Being an independent diligence, there is no requirement that the adjudger should first have inhibited. Decree in the action does not complete the diligence. Just as delivery of a disposition to a purchaser gives him no real right, so an adjudger has no real right by his decree, but must, like a purchaser, complete title by recording in the Sasine Register or registration in the Land Register. In certain cases the decree will be recorded in the Personal Register, but normally this is not necessary. (The title of the Personal Register—the Register of Inhibitions and Adjudications—is misleading in this respect.)

Adjudication gives the adjudger not legal ownership, not the fee of the estate, but only a judicial heritable security. He can remove the debtor, let out the property, and take the rents. But for a period of ten years (called by the odd name of the 'legal') he cannot sell the property. (But if during the legal the property is sold compulsorily, eg by a standard security holder, the adjudger will be paid at once, as a heritable creditor, according to his ranking. Similarly the legal may be cut short by a sequestration or a liquidation.) If by the end of the legal the debt is still unpaid, the adjudger brings an action of declarator of expiry of the legal, which will give him full ownership.

Development of the law. Authorities

The essentials of the law of inhibition and adjudication have changed little since at least the seventeenth century. (For the history of inhibition, see Walter Ross's *Lectures* (1822)). Throughout this period inhibition has been an important part of both conveyancing and court practice. This long continuous history has meant that the law has attained a considerable degree of coherence and certainty. The treatment, therefore, of inhibition by such writers as Stair, Bankton, Erskine and Bell is not merely of antiquarian interest, but can generally be taken as an accurate statement of the modern law, subject only to changes of detail. Bell in his *Commentaries* gave the most authoritative re-statement of the law of inhibition, and his Canons of Ranking (reproduced in chapter 7) are repeatedly cited, and sometimes even read.

Stewart's *Diligence*, published in 1898, has always been regarded as of high authority, although not at the same level as the writers mentioned in the last paragraph. Stewart has a full account of both inhibition and adjudication. Since 1898 there has been no authoritative text. Indeed, since 1898 there has been no complete re-statement of the law at all, whether authoritative or not.

Proposals for reform

The Scottish Law Commission's Report on Diligence and Debtor Protection, with draft Bill attached, was published in 1985. While it does not deal with inhibition and adjudication generally, it does have certain incidental provisions which would alter the law. To implement this Report the government has announced a Debtors (Scotland) Bill for the 1986/7 parliamentary session. At the time of writing it is a matter of speculation whether this will reach the statute book, and if so, in what form.

One minor reform in this Report requires notice, namely that adjudication on a document of debt would become incompetent.

The Commission is continuing to work on the law of diligence and it is expected that within the next few years a further Report will be published which will review inhibition and adjudication in detail and make extensive proposals for reform.

The McKechnie Report (1958, Cmnd 456) and the Grant Report (1967, Cmnd 3248) both recommended that the Sheriff Court be given jurisdiction in inhibition. Though this recommendation has not been implemented as yet, the writer would guess that sooner or later it is sure to reach the statute book. The Halliday Report (1966, Cmnd 3118) recommended that a procedure be introduced whereby a debtor could voluntarily inhibit himself in favour of a chosen creditor, as a sort of security for credit. This would have been called a 'personal charge'. This was not introduced and does not seem to command wide support.

In my study of the law I have naturally formed my own ideas as to possible reform. I shall mention only three points. (1) The difficulties which arise in marrying the law of inhibition with the provisions of the 1979 Act could probably be resolved at a stroke by making inhibition an over-riding interest. (2) Inhibition on the dependence is too easily obtained. As long ago as the eighteenth century, complains Ross (*Lectures*, 1822 ed, 1,468), inhibition on the dependence had come to be used 'for every claim that one man could muster up against another. In this view it is the most cruel and impolitic diligence ever introduced into the law of any country.' Little has changed. Inhibition on the dependence continues to be used to pressurize (or 'concuss' to use the technical word) defenders in an unfair manner. The solution would be a rule whereby inhibition on the dependence would be granted only on cause shown. This is already the law for interdict on the dependence, otherwise known as interim interdict, and it is suggested that much the same law and procedure could be applied to interim inhibition. (The same goes for arrestment on the dependence, but that is another story.) (3) Clearly there is a need to modernise the law of adjudication. My strong opinion is that the mechanism whereby the adjudging creditor becomes formally infeft is a wise one and must be preserved. I am certain that any other solution would be fated to technical disaster.

CHAPTER 2

Creation

Scope of chapter

This chapter deals with the grounds on which, and the procedure by which, an inhibition is obtained, together with certain other incidental matters.

There are three grounds for inhibition. (1) A decree for payment. This is called inhibition in execution. (2) A depending cause. This is called inhibition on the dependence. (If the action is successful, it automatically becomes an inhibition in execution. There is no need for a new inhibition. If the action is unsuccessful, the inhibition automatically lapses.) (3) A document of debt.

The expression 'inhibition in security' is sometimes used as a synonym for inhibition on the dependence. But more strictly it means inhibition used in respect of a debt which is future or contingent at the time of the inhibition. In this book this expression is used in this stricter sense. Inhibition in security is thus a classification which cuts across the classification given in the last paragraph, since any of the three types of inhibition may or may not also be an inhibition in security. The commonest case of inhibition in security is in relation to actions for aliment or divorce.

Inhibition in execution

Inhibition in execution proceeds upon a decree of the Court of Session or the Sheriff Court. Although a decree under the old small debt system was not a ground for inhibition (*Lamont*[1] (1867)), it is thought that it is competent to inhibit in execution of a summary cause decree. (Inhibition is in practice granted on summary cause decrees. See also W. N. McBryde and N. J. Dowie, *Petition Procedure in the Court of Session*, (1980), p 47. The contrary view expressed in Gloag and Henderson's *Introduction to the Law of Scotland*, 8th edn (1979), p 780, is, it is thought, not well

---

1 (1867) 6 M 282.

founded.) Inhibition in execution may be used in execution of deeds competently registered for execution in the Books of Council and Session or (uncommonly nowadays) the Sheriff Court Books, for such deeds become, by virtue of such registration, decrees of the court, technically known as decrees of registration. The deeds which can be so recorded are (a) probative deeds incorporating consent to summary diligence and (b) notarial instruments of protest upon dishonoured negotiable instruments. (The former is by common law. The latter is by the Acts 1681 c 20 (APS c 86), 1696 c 36 (APS c 38), 12 George III c 72 and s 98 of the Bills of Exchange Act 1882.)

Some difficulty exists if the debt is one regulated by the Consumer Credit Act 1974. Under the old legislation (the Moneylenders Acts) summary diligence was incompetent. But the 1974 Act repealed the old legislation and does not appear to have re-enacted the prohibition upon summary diligence. It is possible that a court would take a creative approach and hold that the general policy of the Act is contrary to summary diligence. Section 173(1) of the Act might be appealed to in this context. But until such time as a court does take such a creative approach, the tentative conclusion would seem to be that summary diligence is competent upon a regulated agreement, provided, of course, that the document of debt contains the necessary consent. (I am indebted to Mr R. Bruce Wood for these points.)

An award by an Industrial Tribunal is a ground for inhibition, since such an award is (by a rather odd and perhaps unsatisfactory fiction) deemed to be a degree of registration. See the Employment Protection (Consolidation) Act 1978, Sch 9, para. 7(2). There is a comparable provision in s 12 of the Agricultural Marketing Act 1958.

It is not competent to inhibit on a summary warrant for rates, taxes or Value Added Tax. The legislation makes it clear that the only diligence competent is poinding (and, in the case of rates, arrestment). By the same reasoning as was applied to small debt decrees in *Lamont*[2] (1867) it follows that inhibition is excluded. If therefore it is desired to inhibit in respect of arrears of tax or rates or VAT, it is necessary to raise an action for payment. (The relevant legislation for summary warrants is: Local Government (Scotland) Act 1947, ss 247–249; Taxes Management Act 1970, ss 63–64; Value Added Tax Act 1983 Sch 7(6) and SI 1980/1536.)

Inhibition can be used on decrees of courts outwith Scotland if they have been competently registered here for enforcement under the Civil Jurisdiction and Judgments Act 1982 or other legislation.

---

2 (1867) 6 M 282.

Inhibition on the dependence

Inhibition may be used on the dependence of actions in the Court of Session or the Sheriff Court. In general, it can be said that if inhibition is competent in execution of a decree, it is competent on the dependence of the action. However, it would seem that it is not competent to inhibit on the dependence of an Industrial Tribunal case, even though it is possible to inhibit in execution of the award.

Inhibition on the dependence is normally granted de cursu. It is up to the defender to seek recall if he thinks the inhibition unjustified. (See chapter 3.) If the action is successful, the inhibition will remain in force. If the action is unsuccessful, whether by reason of dismissal or absolvitor, the inhibition is extinguished. (See chapter 3.)

Inhibition on the dependence is sometimes called inhibition 'in security' but it seems preferable to use the latter expression to mean inhibition in respect of a future or contingent debt, irrespective of whether it is in execution or on the dependence or on a document of debt.

Inhibition on a document of debt

It is competent, though nowadays not common, to inhibit on a 'document of debt' even though the creditor does not have decree (even of registration) and there is no depending cause. There seems to be no clear authority as to what counts for this purpose as a document of debt. It is suggested that a suitable definition would be any document whereby the debtor in probative writing binds himself in payment. This would include personal bonds and most leases. At common law bills of exchange were probative (Stair 4.42.6) and accordingly were regarded as documents of debt on which inhibition could proceed. In *McIntyre v National Bank of Scotland*[3] (1910) it was held that bills of exchange are not probative. The decision seems questionable, and thus despite this decision it has continued to be the practice to grant inhibition on bills of exchange (and likewise promissory notes).

The authorities sometimes suggest that the document of debt must be 'liquid'. But strictly this is not necessary. (For a discussion of what is 'liquid' see W. A. Wilson, *Debt* (1982), p 11.) Thus a bill of exchange drawn at ninety days' sight is it seems not 'liquid' before maturity, but it will found inhibition. (For inhibition on future debts, see below.)

3 1910 SC 150.

Usually if a document is a 'document of debt' in the relevant sense it will warrant summary diligence, and of course if the creditor registers it for execution, he will be inhibiting not on the document but on the decree of registration. (In the case of bills and notes what is registered is not the document but the notarial instrument of protest.) It might therefore be thought that there is never any need to inhibit on the document itself. There are, however, two cases where such a need may arise. (a) Where summary diligence cannot be done, because the document does not warrant it. Thus inhibition could be used on a personal bond which omitted the usual consent to summary diligence. The essence of a 'document of debt' is the probative undertaking to pay, and not the right to use summary diligence. (b) Where summary diligence cannot be done, because the debt is not yet due. (Schedule 1 of the Debtors (Scotland) Act 1838 (the Personal Diligence Act) permits decrees of registration for future debts, but it appears to the writer that this Schedule ceased to have effect after s 15 and s 39 of the Administration of Justice (Scotland) Act 1933.) In this latter case the creditor will only wish to inhibit if he has reason to believe that the debt will not be honoured when it falls due. A typical example would be where the creditor holds a bill of exchange at a currency of, say, 90 days. Before maturity it becomes clear that the acceptor is becoming insolvent. In this case the holder could raise an inhibition on his document of debt, ie the accepted bill. The debt still being future, this would be an inhibition in security.

Where inhibition is on a document of debt, procedure is by bill and letters. Recall is by petition.

Inhibition in security: future and contingent debts

As has been explained, the expression 'inhibition in security' is sometimes used to mean inhibition on the dependence, but more strictly it means inhibition in respect of a future or contingent debt. This can arise in connection with any of the three types of inhibition, ie inhibition in execution, inhibition on the dependence and inhibition on a document of debt. The most frequent case is in relation to consistorial causes, and it would appear that all the case law on inhibition in security relates to such causes. However, it can arise outwith the context of consistorial actions. A characteristic example would be the one mentioned earlier, namely inhibition on a bill of exchange prior to maturity.

For the question of what debts are, in the eyes of the law, future or contingent, see W. A. Wilson's *Law of Scotland relating to Debt* (1982) pp 12–17. In particular it is to be observed that sums concluded for in actions of aliment and of divorce are generally to be regarded as future or contingent: see eg *Gillanders*[4] (1966) and *Brash*[5] (1966)..

It is necessary to stress the exceptional nature of diligence in security. It is an exception to the general rule that diligence is competent only in respect of debts presently due and resting owing. Thus Lord Curriehill in *Dove v Henderson*[6] (1865) says that 'according to our law there can be no diligence used to secure future debts in ordinary circumstances'. But, as this quotation itself makes clear, the rule applies only to 'ordinary circumstances'. If 'special circumstances' exist, then diligence in security is possible. What, then, are 'special circumstances'?

In the older authorities, only one such special circumstance was recognised, namely where the debtor was *vergens ad inopiam* (verging on insolvency). This conception does not seem to have been fully defined. The writer conjectures that it is to be equiparated with the concept of practical insolvency as developed in the law of bankruptcy. That is to say, the debtor has de facto ceased to pay his debts as they fall due, regardless of whether or not he is insolvent in absolute terms. (For the basis of this suggested equiparation, see *Campbell v Cullen*[7] (1848). For practical insolvency, see the leading case of *Scottish Milk Marketing Board v Wood*[8] (1936).)

The category of special circumstances was later widened to include the case where the debtor is *in meditatione fugae* (about to decamp). For this, and for the case discussed in the last paragraph, see especially *Symington*[9] (1875), *Burns*[10] (1879), *Smith*[11] (1932) *Beton*[12] (1961) and *Pow*[13] (1986).

In a recent case, *Wilson*[14] (1981), the category of 'special circumstances' was further widened. In this case Lord Maxwell granted to the pursuer warrant to inhibit in respect of the financial conclusions of a divorce action (which, as has been mentioned, are regarded as future or contingent) on the ground that there was evidence that her husband was planning to sell his house and use the money so realised to buy another in the name of his mistress.

---

4 1966 SC 54.
5 1966 SC 56.
6 (1865) 3 M 339.
7 (1848) 10 D 1496.
8 1936 SC 604.
9 (1875) 3 R 205.
10 (1879) 7 R 355.
11 1932 SLT 45.
12 1961 SLT (Notes) 19.
13 1986 GWD 1–7.
14 1981 SLT 101.

Most cases of inhibition in security arise in connection with consistorial causes. The law here is now regulated by s 19 of the Family Law (Scotland) Act 1985, for which see below.

The rule that inhibition in security is permissible only in special circumstances raises the question as to how this rule is to be 'policed'. This question will first be considered at common law, and thereafter in relation to the provisions of s 19 of the Family Law (Scotland) Act 1985.

Where inhibition is sought using the traditional method of bill and letters (see later) it is necessary that the bill should narrate the special circumstances which are founded on. (See the cases mentioned in the preceding paragraphs, and also in particular see *Dove v Henderson*[15] (1865) and *Stevens v Campbell*[16] (1873).) The bill should then be accompanied by any necessary documentary evidence. If this is not done, the fiat will be refused. (In cases of doubt the Clerk should always refuse the fiat, whereupon the matter will go before the Lord Ordinary under RC 189(b). The Lord Ordinary may then grant or refuse the fiat, according to law.)

Where the inhibition is sought by motion in the course of a depending Court of Session action, much the same applies. Special circumstances must be stated, failing which the Lord Ordinary will refuse the motion. It is thought that in this case he must refuse the motion even if it is unopposed.

It is thought that mere averment is not sufficient. It is thought that the party seeking inhibition must make out a prima facie case that the special circumstances stated in fact prevail. Ex parte evidence is sufficient. But it is thought that the Court always has a discretion to refuse, in other words that inhibition in security is a proceeding by way of equity rather than by way of right. It is suggested that there is a close parallel with interim interdict.

The main source of difficulty as to 'policing' arises when warrant to inhibit is sought as part of the Court of Session summons. Here there exists no machinery to ensure that inhibition is not granted unlawfully.

The practice (approved by Lord Ashmore in *Noble*[17] (1921)) is that in such a case the summons itself contains averments as to the special circumstances. But the law here is defective. There is no system whereby prima facie evidence can be led to support the averments. Nor is there any procedure (unlike the case of bills) whereby the matter can be referred to the Lord Ordinary. The problem can best be expressed by putting it into the somewhat antiquated language of traditional pro-

---

15 (1865) 3 M 339.
16 (1873) 11 M 772.
17 1921 1 SLT 57.

cedure: letters of summons, unlike other letters passing the signet, require no fiat. They go direct to signeting without a prior fiat. In this connection it is necessary to observe that signeting is not done by the Court of Session itself. It is done by those holding commission to that effect from the Keeper of the Signet. Since 1976 this commission has in fact been given to certain clerks of the Court, but when they act it is as deputies of the Keeper and not as clerks of the Court. (Prior to 1976 signeting was done by writers to the signet, a system which is reverted to during civil service strikes. It is important to notice that signeting of Court of Session writs is fundamentally a different process from the warranting of Sheriff Court writs. Warranting is done by or on behalf of the Sheriff, whereas signeting is by the Crown and not by the Lords of Council and Session at all. Hence the problem.)

The problem was touched on by Lord Maxwell in *Wilson*[18] (1981) where he suggested that a summons seeking warrant to inhibit in security but not containing the necessary averments should be refused the signet. This is sensible, but it is not clear to what extent those holding the commission for the signet have the power to refuse signeting. It would be different if they could, in cases of doubt, refer the matter to the Lord Ordinary, but as far as the writer is aware, this is not competent.

A similar difficulty arises in connection with applications for warrant to inhibit on the dependence of actions which have no pecuniary conclusions except for expenses. As is mentioned below, inhibition in such cases is generally incompetent. But how is this rule to be policed? The reader is referred to the eloquent lament of Sheriff Fyfe in *Van Uden v Burrell*[19] (1914). In this case it was an arrestment which was in question, but in this area there is little difference between arrestment and inhibition. It should be added that in the Sheriff Court it is at least in theory possible for the Sheriff to instruct the clerk to refuse the warrant in cases of doubt, and to refer the matter to him for consideration. This is because, as mentioned above, warranting of Sheriff Court writs is, in theory, by or on behalf of the Sheriff. Signeting is different.

If, for whatever reason, an inhibition in security is laid on without justification, the remedy is recall, as described in the next chapter.

Consistorial causes

Section 19 of the Family Law (Scotland) Act 1985 provides that inhibition may be used in connection with actions for aliment and divorce 'on cause shown'. The effect of this provision falls to be

18 1981 SLT 101.
19 1914 SLT 411.

considered both substantively and procedurally. Substantively it is thought that it effects no change in the law. Prior to 1985, as has been explained, inhibition in relation to such actions was in any case regarded as inhibition in security and therefore permissible only in 'special circumstances'. It is thought that s 19 is, from a substantive point of view, little more than a statutory recognition of this rule. On this view the existing body of case law as to what can count as 'special circumstances' will continue to be applicable. A different view, however, is taken by H. R. M. Macdonald in his *Guide to the Family Law (Scotland) Act 1985* (1986) where he says (p 61) that s 19 will make it easier to obtain inhibition.

The procedural effect of s 19 is, to the writer, more doubtful. One possible interpretation would be that the pursuer needs only to make relevant averments, failing which the summons should be refused the signet, or the bill refused the fiat, or the motion refused. Thus in the case of warrant sought as part of the summons, it will be the duty of those holding the commission to inspect the summons and make the appropriate decision. This seems not absolutely satisfactory, since, as has already been said, the writer knows of no procedure whereby issues of signeting can be referred to the Lord Ordinary in cases of doubt. The other interpretation would be that 'cause shown' means cause shown to the Court. This seems a more reasonable construction of the expression. But it would seem to have the necessary consequence that a summons of this nature could not include warrant to inhibit. Procedure would have to be by bill or motion, so as to enable the matter to be put before the Lord Ordinary. Against this construction it has to be said that for such a signal change in the law one would have expected clearer statutory language, plus reference to the Court of Session Act 1868, which first introduced the system of seeking warrant to inhibit as part of the summons. Between these two interpretations, the writer feels ill-qualified to decide. But, for all its difficulties, he tentatively prefers the second, as being more rational in its effect. On this view the pursuer would, it is thought, have to make, not merely relevant averments, but also a prima facie case, and discretion would lie in the Court.

Must the claim be pecuniary?

The general rule is that inhibition is competent only upon a pecuniary claim. Thus it is not competent to inhibit on the dependence of a purely declaratory action. This rule cannot be circumvented by arguing that the inhibition is in respect of the expenses concluded for. (See *Weir v Otto*[20] (1870).) However, once expenses have been decerned for, it is

20 (1870) 8 M 1070.

competent to inhibit for them, even though they arose out of a declaratory action. (See the judgment of Lord Cowan in the case just mentioned. See also *Wilkie v Tweeddale*[1] (1815) where a successful defender was allowed to inhibit in respect of untaxed expenses and *Jack v McCaig*[2] (1880).)

For the problem of how the rule against inhibition on non-pecuniary claims is to be 'policed', see above.

Exceptions to the general rule do exist. In particular it appears to be competent to inhibit where the action relates to the defender's heritable property, as in an action to enforce a contract of sale, or of lease. See *Barstow v Menzies*[3] (1840) and *Seaforth Trustees v Macaulay*[4] (1844). But it must be said that the law here is in an undeveloped state. It is odd that in such a case the inhibition strikes at all the defender's heritage, rather than just the property in question.

Under the Family Law (Scotland) Act 1985, ss 8 and 19, it is competent to inhibit in respect of a property transfer order. The Court is empowered to restrict the inhibition to the property in question. The Law Society of Scotland had urged that the order should itself be directly registrable in the Personal Register, but this proposal was not adopted. (See further Colin B. Miller's papers to the PQLE Course on Conveyancing, December 1986, at pages 131–133 of the Conference papers. Mr Miller recommends that inhibition should always be resorted to in this type of case.)

Caution by inhibitor

In the case of inhibition on the dependence and, probably, inhibition on a document of debt, the Court may require the applicant to find caution for damages claimable by the other party in the event that the inhibition proves to be wrongous. (For damages for wrongous use, see below.) There is, however, very little authority on the point. For instance, Stewart says nothing of it, though he does point out at p 199 that an arrester can be required to find caution. On a point of this sort, inhibition and arrestment tend to be the same. One example where caution has been required of an inhibitor is *Barstow v Menzies*[5] (1840). Whether the Court might be able to impose this requirement ex proprio motu, or whether there must be a motion or petition to that effect by the inhibited party, is unclear.

1 25 Feb 1815 Fac Coll.
2 (1880) 7 R 465.
3 28 Jan 1840 Fac Dec.
4 (1844) 7 D 180.
5 28 Jan 1840 Fac Dec.

Procedure by bill and letters

Formerly bill and letters were the only means of obtaining warrant to inhibit. Even today they remain the only means in all cases but one. The one exception is the case of inhibition on the dependence of a Court of Session action. In that case warrant to inhibit is obtained either as part of the summons, or by motion. (It is thought that there would be nothing to stop the pursuer using bill and letters if he so wished, but in practice there would be no reason to do so.) In other cases, it is necessary to proceed by bill and letters. These cases, therefore, are: (1) inhibition in execution of a Court of Session decree, in the event that inhibition was not already obtained while the cause was in dependence; (2) inhibition on a document of debt; (3) inhibition on the dependence of a Sheriff Court action, or in execution of a Sheriff Court decree.

Bill and letters of inhibition are merely part of the old system of Signet Letters, once an important part of Court of Session procedure. They are the only such letters now in common use, for the other forms of Signet Letters, such as letters of horning and letters of arrestment, though never abolished, have long been out of common use, chiefly as a consequence of the reforms brought about by the Personal Diligence Act 1838. (The official short title is the Debtors (Scotland) Act 1838.) Since 1838 decrees contain a warrant for diligence. Before 1838 this was not so. If, after decree, the debtor did not pay, the creditor had to make a fresh application to the Court for warrant to use diligence. He did this by a bill (in effect a sort of petition, whence it is that bills are now dealt with in the Petition Department, which has taken over the functions of the Bill Chamber). The granting of the bill by the Court authorised the signeting of the letters. Thus if the creditor wished to arrest, he would present a bill for arrestment, which would receive the fiat from the Bill Chamber, present the letters of arrestment to the Signet Office, which, seeing the fiat on the bill, would signet the letters. The signeted letters were then warrant to arrest. The 1838 Act introduced our modern system of incorporating warrant for diligence in the decree itself, thus short-cutting the entire bill and letters system.

For reasons which are unclear, the reform which was felt to be desirable for poinding and arrestment was not felt to be desirable for inhibition. Remarkably, nothing has been done since 1838 to complete the reform, so that inhibitions still require (in most cases) the pre-1838 method of bill and letters.

The first step is to prepare the bill for letters of inhibition. This is signed by the applicant's law agent, and is presented to the Petition Department of the Court of Session, which, as mentioned, now discharges the functions of the old Bill Chamber. The bill narrates the grounds on which inhibition is sought. In particular, it will specify the decree or depending cause or document of debt on which the applicant founds. In the case of inhibition in security the bill should aver the special circumstances which justify it (see p 11 above). The documentation narrated in the bill must be produced. In the case of inhibition on the dependence of a Sheriff Court action the practice is to require the copy writ certified by the Sheriff Clerk or his depute, together with evidence of service.

Assuming that the bill is properly framed and is supported by the relevant documentation, the bill is granted. In cases of doubt the matter is referred to the Lord Ordinary (succeeding to the functions of the old Lord Ordinary on the Bills) in terms of RC 189(b). His decision cannot be reclaimed. The mode of granting the bill is for the clerk to write on it: '*Fiat ut petitur*, because the Lords have seen the extract decree.' (These last words will be suitably changed in the case of inhibition on the dependence or on a document of debt.) The bill is then said to have received the fiat.

The bill bearing the fiat constitutes authority for the letters to pass the signet. The letters, which are prepared by the applicant, run in the name of the Crown, and must be in the statutory form (Schedule QQ of the 1868 Act). The substance of the letters will of course conform to the substance of the bill.

The signeted letters constitute warrant to inhibit. The actual inhibition is effected by service and recording. But before considering how the inhibition is served and recorded, it is necessary first to deal with the methods of obtaining warrant to inhibit without recourse to the bill and letters procedure.

Procedure without bill and letters

In the case of inhibition on the dependence of a Court of Session action, but in no other case, it is possible to obtain warrant to inhibit without bill and letters.

(1) Summons

By the Court of Session Act 1868, and RC 74, it is competent to apply for warrant to inhibit in the summons itself, so that the signeting of the summons has the same effect as the signeting of letters of inhibition. This procedure is very common. It has already been pointed out that this procedure has the unfortunate effect of excluding judicial scrutiny at the time of granting.

(2) Motion

RC 74(d) provides that warrant to inhibit can be obtained by motion before the Lord Ordinary. This will of course apply only where warrant was not obtained as part of the summons, as above. This procedure is available only so long as the cause is depending. If there has been no inhibition on the dependence and it is desired to inhibit in execution, this procedure is unavailable, and it is necessary to resort to bill and letters. Where warrant to inhibit is obtained by motion, the certified copy interlocutor takes the position of signeted letters. It scarcely needs to be said that the motion must be enrolled and intimated in the usual way. The practice is that the motion is starred even if unopposed.

(3) Additional defenders

It is competent to apply for warrant to inhibit in a Minute of Amendment citing additional defenders: RC 74(f).

(4) Third party procedure

Warrant to inhibit may be included in the order authorising a Third Party Notice: RC 85(b). Under this procedure, it is the first defender, not the pursuer, who is the inhibitor.

(5) Counterclaim

It is competent to inhibit on the dependence of a counterclaim, the application being included in the counterclaim itself: RC 84(c).

(6) Consequential points

A theoretical point of interest arising is that the old definition of inhibition, that it was a diligence passing the signet (see eg Erskine 2.11.2 or Bell, *Principles*, 2306), though it is still sometimes quoted, is no longer strictly accurate.

It is thought that in all these cases it would still be competent to use the bill and letters procedure, though it is unlikely that there would be any reason to wish to do so.

As was seen earlier, warrant to inhibit as part of the summons (case 1 above) has the unfortute effect of excluding judicial scrutiny at the time of granting. The same appears to be true of cases 3 and 5. But in cases 2 and 4 there would appear to be room for judicial scrutiny. In this connection see *Fisher v Weir*[6] (1964). This case considered RC 74(d)—or rather its predecessor—in connection with arrestment, but the distinction for present purposes is immaterial. Lord Kilbrandon said:

6 1964 SLT (Notes) 99.

'The pursuer's attitude is, that since a warrant to arrest could have been inserted in the summons, she must be entitled to have one granted some four months later. That may be literally so, but it is now known that the warrant is to be opposed, and it would be a very absurd situation if I were to hold myself bound to grant today a warrant which I could see good reasons for recalling tomorrow.'

Lord Kilbrandon went on to refuse the pursuer's motion, on condition that the defender consigned that part of the sum sued for which he (the defender) admitted was due. (The rule is—see next chapter—that a defender is entitled to have an inhibition (or arrestment) on the dependence recalled on consignation of the sum sued for or such part thereof as the Court shall provide.) The tendency of this decision is in the direction of allowing inhibition on the dependence only causa cognita. That would represent a change from the present law, but in the opinion of the author it would be a beneficial change.

Service

It is necessary that the inhibition be served on the debtor. This is done by messenger at arms, whose warrant is the letters of inhibition (or other warrant, as described earlier). He serves both the warrant (thus where the warrant is contained in a summons it is necessary to serve the summons: see Stewart, p 540) and a schedule of inhibition. Service is personal, or at the dwelling house, or edictal. It is thought that an agent cannot accept service. Postal service appears not to be competent. (Stewart, p 40. Maxwell's *Practice of the Court of Session* (1980), p 181. See also Schedule QQ of the 1868 Act. There has been speculation that RC74A in its present form authorises postal service, but the writer considers the law to be unchanged.) Upon service the messenger at arms returns to the inhibitor the execution of inhibition. The inhibitor requires the execution as proof of service. Without this proof the inhibition cannot be recorded.

Service by sheriff officer is competent only in the exceptional case provided by s 1 of the Execution of Diligence (Scotland) Act 1926.

Special parties

For special parties such as partnerships, trustees and so on, reference is made to chapter 5. In some cases (eg a body of trustees) difficult questions can arise as to what constitutes competent service of the inhibition. But it is thought that this is simply a part of the general law relating to service and that there are no particular specialities which apply to inhibitions.

Executry

The effect of the death of the inhibited party is considered in chapter 3. The question to be considered here is inhibition by a creditor of the defunct against the executor. The law on this question is undeveloped, chiefly because at common law the heritable estate was not administered by the executor. Subject to certain qualifications, the administration of the heritable estate by the executor was first brought in by Succession (Scotland) Act 1964.

Diligence against the executor by a creditor of the defunct is in general not competent for six months from the date of death. Section 14 of the Act of 1964 can be read as applying this general rule to inhibitions, but in the absence of express authority or clear principle the matter cannot be regarded as free from doubt.

Since an executor in certain cases can dispose of the heritable estate without confirmation (see the well-known opinion of the Professors of Conveyancing published at (1965) 10 JLSS 153), it is presumably competent to inhibit an unconfirmed executor.

Procedure is by raising an action against the executor and inhibiting on the dependence. If the creditor already holds a decree against the defunct, or holds a document of debt, it might be argued that this sufficed for inhibition against the executor, by bill and letters, without raising any action. If this were the case, the creditor would naturally have to present with the bill evidence identifying the executor as such. The writer is not able to express a concluded view on the competency of such procedure.

Recording the inhibition

The language of the execution of the inhibition (see chapter 14) indicates that the debtor is inhibited from the time of execution. This is not so: the style of the execution of inhibition reflects the pre-1868 law, according to which the inhibition took effect from service, subject to the condition that it be recorded within 40 days. But by s 155 of the 1868 Act, and s 18 of the Court of Session Act 1868, an inhibition takes effect not from service but from recording. An unrecorded inhibition is of no effect, even as against parties who have knowledge of it.

The appropriate register is the Register of Inhibitions and Adjudications at Edinburgh. This register is in practice called the Personal Register (sometimes also the 'Diligence Register'), and is so referred to in this book. But it should be understood that this name has no official standing, and the correct name should always be used in framing writs and deeds. The Personal Register has a long history, but in its present form it is based on s 44 of the 1924 Act. The register is kept at

Meadowbank House, 153 London Road, tel 661 6111. The department which keeps the register is called 'Hornings'. This curious name derives from the fact that it also keeps the Register of Hornings, though this latter register is now obsolete in practice.

Entries in the register are said to be 'recorded' or 'registered'. Both usages are correct.

The Keeper is entitled to refuse to accept inhibitions which he deems invalid. But if he does so wrongfully he may be liable in damages. See *Davidson v Mackenzie*[7] (1856).

Time from which effective

Section 155 of the 1868 Act provides that an inhibition takes effect from the date of recording. If there is also a Notice recorded the effect is backdated to the date of the Notice, but only if not more than 21 days have elapsed from the date of the Notice.

Two questions arise in this connection. The first is as to the calculation of the 21 days. The wording of the Act is 'not later than twenty-one days from the date of the registration . . .'. It is thought that this means that if the Notice is recorded on 1 October then the last day for recording the inhibition (if it is to have the benefit of backdating) is 22 October.

The other question arises when an act which would be struck at by the inhibition occurs on the same day as the inhibition takes effect. Section 155, as has been seen, speaks only of the 'date' and says nothing of the actual time of recording. The Register of Sasines Act 1693 (c 23) made provision for the actual time of recording to enter the Register of Inhibitions, but this provision was repealed by s 29(3) of the 1979 Act, with the result that now only the date is noted. As a consequence, the actual time of recording cannot be relevant. The law must deem the inhibition to take effect at some fixed time, regardless of when it was actually recorded. This might be the beginning of the day, or the end of the day, or some arbitrary time during the course of the day. It is difficult to devise any solution which would not, in some circumstances, work injustice to the inhibitor or to a third party. On balance, however, the least bad solution would seem to be that the inhibition should be deemed to take effect from the end of the day, subject to the proviso that a third party will nevertheless be affected if in bad faith. But this is no more than a conjecture.

The ordinary name of the register, the Personal Register, casts light on its nature, for it is a register of persons and not of property. To discover whether a given person is inhibited, the procedure is simply to

7 (1856) 19 D 226.

make a search of the indices. These are now computerised. In the Personal Register are also recorded writs extinguishing and restricting inhibitions, ie discharges, decrees and certified copy interlocutors of recall. (For these, see next chapter.) A fee is payable for all entries in the register, and for searches. Extracts of entries in the register can be issued, but in practice there is rarely any need for them.

What is actually recorded in the Personal Register is (a) the warrant, ie the letters of inhibition, or other warrants (such as Court of Session summons containing warrant for inhibition) as detailed at p 17 above, and (b) the execution of inhibition, which is returned after service by the messenger at arms to the inhibitor. Like the Sasine Register, but unlike the Books of Council and Session, the originals are returned to the party.

The Personal Register is not only a 'public register' (ie open to the public for inspection) but also a 'register for publication'. This means that its contents are deemed to be known to all parties having an interest. (In this respect the Personal Register is like the Sasine Register.) The status of the Personal Register as a register for publication was confirmed by s 18 of the Court of Session Act 1868, which provides that upon recording, an inhibition 'shall be held to be duly intimated and published to all concerned'.

Notice of inhibition

As stated above an inhibition takes effect on the date of its recording. To this rule there exists one important exception. Prior to recording his inhibition, and prior even to its service, the inhibitor may record in the Personal Register a Notice of Inhibition. If the inhibition is itself recorded no more than 21 days thereafter, the inhibition is deemed to take effect as at the date of the Notice. If the inhibition is not recorded, or is recorded outwith the 21-day period, the Notice is of no effect. Procedure is regulated by s 155 of the 1868 Act. It should be noted that it is important that the Notice should correspond with the terms of its warrant (ie the letters or summons). If it does not it will not be accepted by the Keeper.

The section just cited provides for the Notice procedure where the inhibition proceeds on letters of inhibition or on a Court of Session summons containing warrant to inhibit. In 1868 these were the only two competent warrants for inhibition. On a literal reading of the section, therefore, the Notice procedure is not available where warrant to inhibit is obtained in neither of these two ways.

The purpose of the Notice procedure is to give the inhibitor the advantages of celerity and surprise, in circumstances where delay, or warning to the debtor, may prove fatal. While there is clearly a strong case for such procedure, it should be observed that the effect is that a debtor may be inhibited several days before he is de facto aware of the fact. This can lead to injustice.

Where the Notice procedure is used, the inhibition may commence before the action is served. Since a cause does not formally begin to depend until the moment of service, the paradoxical result is that there can (for a few days) be an inhibition on the dependence which is on the dependence of nothing. (A similar point applies in the law of arrestment.) But the paradox seems to be merely a verbal one. Strictly we would have to say that an inhibition before service is not an inhibition on the dependence, but sui generis.

The Land Register

Section 6(1) (c) of the 1979 Act directs the Keeper to enter on each title sheet in the Land Register 'any subsisting entry in the Register of Inhibitions and Adjudications adverse to the interest'. This is a sensible provision, but it appears to the writer that the Act fails to provide the technical framework necessary. Serious technical problems would seem to result from this.

Three points must be noted at the outset. The first is that the Keeper 'shall' make such entries. The second is that inhibition is not an 'overriding interest'. The third is that it is understood that the practice at Register House is that inhibitions are not inserted in the title sheet as soon as they appear in the Personal Register. Instead, it is only when something happens which triggers an updating of the title sheet that the Personal Register is checked and relevant entries are noted. Thus in practice an inhibition will often stand in the Personal Register for a considerable period before the title sheet is changed. In many cases (where nothing has happened to trigger updating) the inhibition will not find its way to the title sheet at all.

The first difficulty

The first problem is that whereas the Land Register is a register of infeftments, inhibition strikes not at infeftments but at beneficial interests. In a majority of cases, of course, infeftment and beneficial interest coincide. But in many cases they do not. The fact that X is infeft does not imply that an inhibition against X is effective. Conversely, the fact that Y is uninfeft does not imply that an inhibition against him will be ineffective. An everyday example of the latter is where Y holds land on a docket under s 15 of the Succession (Scotland) Act 1964. An inhibition against Y is effective notwithstanding that Y is not yet infeft.

When an updating happens, the Keeper will very often be put in possession of the necessary information as to beneficial interest. It all depends on what the trigger is, and on how complete the information supplied is. In many cases the Keeper must find himself in the position that he cannot reliably 'marry' the entries in the Personal Register with title sheets in the Land Register. This is not his fault. In the writer's experience the Register House staff are admirably efficient public servants. The fault is in the Act.

The second difficulty

The second problem is that cases arise from time to time where the legal effect of a given inhibition is uncertain. The Keeper is thereby subjected to an unfair responsibility. He must make an essentially judicial decision. That of itself is perhaps acceptable, for the whole system of registration of title involves the Keeper in making quasi-judicial decisions. The problem is that he apparently cannot protect himself by the usual mechanism of exclusion of indemnity.

The third difficulty

The third difficulty is the most serious. When does an inhibition take effect in relation to subjects in the Land Register? This question is all-important, for the effect of an inhibition largely turns upon the date when it legally takes effect.

Section 3 of the 1979 Act provides that a registered title is subject only to such rights as are entered upon the title sheet, apart from overriding interests. It follows that until such time as an inhibition is entered upon the title sheet, it does not affect the interest in question. Thus suppose that A is the registered owner of Blackacre. On 15 May 1987 he is inhibited. On 11 October 1987 he concludes missives to sell Blackacre to B. A Form 12 application is then made. (Report over registered subjects: see the Land Registration (Scotland) Rules 1980).) This application triggers an updating of the title sheet. The inhibition is duly entered on the title sheet on 29 October 1987. At what date does the inhibition take effect in relation to Blackacre? A literal reading of the 1979 Act leads to the conclusion that the relevant date is 29 October 1987. But in that case the inhibition does not stop the sale to B. This conclusion seems unacceptable.

Even if Register House practice were altered so that entries in the Personal Register were at once noted in the relevant title sheet, the problem would still exist in a number of cases, due to the difficulties, mentioned above, of 'marrying' the one register with the other. But in any case it is thought that it would be unworkable from an administrative point of view if the Register House staff had to adopt a procedure based on immediate transfer.

There does not seem to be any discussion of this problem in the literature, except for a short passage in Professor J. M. Halliday's *Conveyancing Law and Practice* (1986, Vol 2, p 448). Here Professor Halliday says that 'if the Keeper by mistake omits to enter in the title sheet an inhibition ... the position appears to be that the inhibitor cannot enforce his rights' on account of s 3 of the Act. 'In such circumstances,' he continues, 'it would appear that the inhibitor may claim to be indemnified by the Keeper for any resulting loss, the Keeper being entitled to subrogation to the inhibitor's rights.' This passage addresses itself to the problem of complete failure to make the entry. Professor Halliday understandably expresses himself in somewhat tentative language. The passage does not deal with the other problem, that of late entry.

The fourth difficulty

The fourth difficulty is less important. It is the problem of what happens if the Keeper notes an inhibition on a title sheet when it should not have been so noted. This might happen by mere human error. Or it might happen because from the information available to the Keeper at the time the entry was correct, whereas fuller information, not then available, would have made the position clear.

The problem here is the same as above, but in the converse. Section 3(1) (c) prima facie appears to mean that the inhibition is effective notwithstanding the error. This seems unacceptable. The error would, perhaps, then be an 'inaccuracy' capable of correction under s 9. But that in turn would lead to the unacceptable result that the inhibitor would be entitled to compensation under s 12.

Assessment

With considerable hesitation, the writer suggests that a literal reading of s 3 of the 1979 Act must be rejected. It is tentatively submitted that an inhibition takes effect when registered in the Personal Register regardless of the date when it is noted in the Land Register, or even if it is not noted at all. This approach is based on four considerations.

The first, very general, consideration is that the 1979 Act must be read in a liberal, constructive way, rather than literalistically. This is because technical flaws can be found elsewhere in the Act. The best known of these is to be found in s 2. Subsection (2) provides that the creation or transfer of a long lease will trigger registration. Subsection (3) provides that subsection (2) does not apply to incorporeal heritable rights. But a long lease is an incorporeal heritable right. Errors like these must be got round by constructive interpretation. It seems reasonable to do the same for inhibitions.

In the second place, it seems to the writer that a literal approach will, in very many cases, be unfair to the Keeper and unfair to inhibitors. Indeed, if the considerations stated above are correct, a literal approach would be unworkable.

In the third place, the Act does not exhibit any intention to make a substantive change in the law of inhibition. The law is presumed not to be altered by mere inadvertence. In particular the Act leaves in force s 18 of the Court of Session Act 1868 and s 155 of the Titles to Land Consolidation (Scotland) Act 1868, which provide that an inhibition is to take effect on the date when it appears in the Personal Register. The 1979 Act could have amended these provisions. It did not do so.

It may be said that a later Act prevails over an earlier one. This is true, but equally it is true that *generalia specialibus non derogant*.

In the fourth place, the 1979 Act itself at one point appears to contemplate that an inhibition may be effective against registered subjects notwithstanding that it has not been entered in the title sheet. The provision is s 12(3) (k). This says that the Keeper is not to pay compensation where

'the loss arises as a result of an error or omission in an office copy as to the effect of any subsisting adverse entry in the Register of Inhibitions and Adjudications affecting any person in respect of any registered interest in land, and that person's entitlement to that interest is neither disclosed in the register nor otherwise known to the Keeper.'

(See further the *Registration of Title Practice Handbook* paragraphs C.80 and F.26). An example of the sort of situation contemplated by this provision is as follows. X is the legatee of Blackacre. Blackacre is registered property. The subjects are docketed to X by the executor under s 15 of the Succession (Scotland) Act 1964. X does not complete title. X is then inhibited. An office copy of the title sheet is issued to Y under s 6(5) of the 1979 Act. This may in practice not disclose the inhibition, for the simple reason that the office copy is a straight copy of the title sheet, and the title sheet will not show the inhibition because the Keeper will very likely not know of X's interest.

On the literalistic approach, this provision would seem unnecessary, for an inhibition, on that view, can never affect registered property until it is itself registered. This provision therefore seems to contemplate the possibility that an inhibition may be effectual against a registered interest even though it does not appear on the title sheet.

The writer's tentative conclusion is therefore that the law continues to be that an inhibition takes effect on the date when it is registered in the Personal Register.

Transmission

An inhibition can be assigned together with the debt to which it relates, and will in fact be deemed to pass even if the assignation fails to refer to it. If the inhibitor dies, the inhibition is unaffected, and will pass to the executry estate together with the debt to which it relates, and thence to the beneficiaries. There is no requirement that the assignation (or confirmation etc) be recorded in the Personal Register, and indeed such recording would appear to be incompetent. (See further Stewart, pp 552–553.)

Renewal

It will be seen in the following chapter that an inhibition prescribes in five years. Prior to the 1924 Act it was possible to avoid this prescription by renewing the inhibition in terms of s 42 of the Conveyancing (Scotland) Act 1874. This provision was repealed by s 44(6) of the 1924 Act, and was not replaced by any provision with comparable effect.

It might therefore be argued that the effect of s 44(6) of the 1924 Act is that a prescribed inhibition cannot in any manner be renewed or restored. But it is thought that the better view is that the creditor is free to inhibit de novo. In other words, it is not competent to renew an inhibition, but it is competent to re-inhibit. W. W. McBryde and N. J. Dowie at p 48 of their *Petition Procedure in the Court of Session* (1980) say that an inhibition may be 'renewed'. If by this is meant re-inhibition, their view is the same as the one here expressed. The distinction between a renewal and a re-inhibition may appear nugatory, but important consequences may follow. Thus on one view of the law, a renewal does, but a re-inhibition does not, keep alive the right to reduce transactions in breach of the first inhibition. (See chapter 3.) In addition there are, of course, procedural differences between renewal and re-inhibition.

From a practical point of view it is sometimes advisable to re-inhibit. There are two cases where this is so. The first is where the inhibition has prescribed, or is about to prescribe. The second is where it is possible that the debtor has acquired heritable property since the date of the inhibition. The reason for this is that inhibition does not affect property acquired after the date of the inhibition. A second inhibition is therefore necessary to catch such property. (See further chapter 4.)

Expenses

It appears that the expenses of using inhibition cannot be recovered from the debtor, irrespective of whether it is used in execution of a decree or not. See Stewart, pp 554–555, and see also *Clark v Scott & Connell*[8] (1878). It is not easy to see that this rule has any rational foundation.

However, where inhibition is used in execution or on the dependence, it does cover not only the principal sum and interest but also the expenses decerned for or to be decerned for. See Bell, 2137 and *Ewing v McClelland*[9] (1860). Where the only pecuniary claim is for expenses (eg a declarator) inhibition cannot be used on the dependence but it can be used in execution of the decree for expenses. This is equally true of a decree of absolvitor or dismissal decerning for expenses in favour of the defender. See *Wilkie v Tweedale*[10] (1815), *Jack v McCaig*[11] (1880) and *Muckarsie v Williamson*[12] (1824).

Quasi-inhibitions

As well as inhibition proper, there are certain other notices which may be inserted in the Personal Register which operate as inhibitions. These are discussed in chapter 12.

8 (1878) 1 Guthrie's Sel Cas 204.
9 (1860) 22 D 1347.
10 25 Feb 1815 Fac Coll.
11 (1880) 7 R 465.
12 (1824) 2 S 771.

CHAPTER 3

Extinction

Scope of chapter

This chapter considers how inhibitions are extinguished, together with certain incidental matters. How the methods of extinction are classified is to some extent an arbitrary matter. This chapter will consider inhibitions as being extinguished in six ways: (1) by payment; (2) by discharge; (3) by recall; (4) by 'lapse'; (5) by death; (6) by prescription. For the effect on inhibition of sequestration, liquidation and receivership, see chapters 10 and 11.

Restriction

Extinction may be total or partial. In the latter case it is termed restriction. Restriction is possible in two of the six cases, namely discharge and recall. Restriction may take one of two forms. In the first place, it may restrict the inhibition so that it is extinguished in relation to certain property while continuing in effect against other property. (This may be done either by a general release, subject to specified exceptions, or by specific release.) In the second place, the restriction may relate to a single specified transaction, the property remaining subject to the inhibition in regard to other transactions. Thus an inhibition might be restricted so as to permit a standard security over specified subjects, the subjects remaining subject to the inhibition in all other respects.

Extinction and the Personal Register

In the case of extinction by prescription and by death, there will be no entry in the Personal Register. In the former case, the fact of extinction appears from the face of the register itself, since five years will have elapsed since the inhibition was created. In the case of death the lack of an entry does not matter, for the debtor being unable to grant debts and deeds, the inhibition can no longer be violated.

There are two methods of recording the extinction. One is for the deed or decree or certified copy interlocutor to be recorded. This was originally incompetent (see eg Ross's *Lectures* (1822), 1.499), but in the course of the nineteenth century this rule fell into desuetude. The other (and original) method is 'scoring'. The deed or decree or interlocutor is presented to the Keeper, who does not record it, but uses it as authority to 'score' the original entry, ie mark it as extinguished. Either method is therefore competent. However, in modern practice scoring is no longer done. It is usual in discharges and decrees and interlocutors to insert a clause authorising scoring, but this was never necessary even when scoring was in use, and so is today doubly pointless.

There seems to be no authority on the point, but it is thought that the entry in the Personal Register is merely evidential of the extinction, rather than constitutive of it. In other words it is thought that a discharge takes effect on delivery, and a decree or interlocutor on granting (and becoming final), even without recording. In practice of course the debtor will wish the extinction to be recorded, and there can be no doubt that a purchaser would be entitled to refuse a title whose validity involved an unrecorded extinction. The only exception to this latter proposition is where the extinction is recorded in the Sasine Register. This occurs where a disposition (etc) bears the executed concurrence of the inhibitor, thereby extinguishing the inhibition quoad that transaction.

It is thought that once an extinctive entry has been made in the Presentment Book of the Personal Register, it cannot be removed.

Extinction and the Land Register

For the relation of the Personal Register to the Land Register, see chapter 2. Although there is provision for entering inhibitions on to the Land Register, there is no provision for entering discharges etc. Presumably such favourable entries can be made under s 6(1) (g) of the 1979 Act.

Payment

Inhibition is extinguished by payment. It is then said to be 'purged'. In exchange for payment the debtor is entitled to receive a discharge of the inhibition. In the absence of agreement to the contrary, he must pay the inhibitor's law agent's fee for this, and, of course, the recording fee. If the inhibitor fails to grant a discharge on these terms, the debtor is entitled to judicial recall. Since such a recall will have been rendered necessary by the inhibitor's wrongful refusal to grant a discharge, the expenses of the recall fall on the inhibitor (except for the recording dues). See *Robertson v Park Dobson & Co*[1] (1896) and *Milne v Birrell*[2] (1902).

Discharge

Usually a discharge merely evidences extinction that has already occurred by payment or lapse. But it may be that the discharge is granted for some other reason. The practice is that the discharge is drafted by the debtor's law agent and revised by the inhibitor's. In general the debtor must pay the inhibitor's law agent's fee. But where a discharge is granted by reason of lapse (see below), the inhibitor must pay both parties' fees. The same rules apply to the recording dues.

In practice the discharge is always attested. It is thought that for recording purposes it should be probative, so that a holograph discharge, which is strictly speaking not probative, would not suffice. But a holograph discharge would certainly found a petition for recall. Whether a discharge neither attested nor holograph would have any status is unclear.

Formerly discharges fell to be stamped at 50p, but since nineteenth March 1985 they have been exempt from duty (Finance Act 1985, s 85).

As already mentioned, a discharge may be partial. In that case it will exempt a certain specified property from the inhibition, or discharge the inhibition entirely under certain exceptions. Alternatively it may release not a property but a transaction, eg the granting of a specified standard security. In the latter case an alternative to a deed of discharge is for the inhibitor to execute his concurrence on the standard security or disposition etc. This is sufficient provided that the deed is recorded in the Sasine Register.

Recall

Recall is the judicial discharge of an inhibition. Recall of inhibition is a Court of Session process, the Sherrif having no jurisdiction in inhibitions.

As mentioned above partial recall (restriction) is competent. For an example, see *McInally v Kildonan Homes Ltd*[3] (1979).

Petition

The traditional means of recall is by petition. This is still necessary in many cases, including all inhibitions on documents of debt, all inhibi-

---

1 (1896) 24 R 30.
2 (1902) 4 F 879.

tions arising out of Sheriff Court actions (whether on the dependence or in execution), and all inhibitions in execution of Court of Session decrees. In other words, the alternatives to petition, namely motion and letter of application, apply only in the case of inhibitions on the dependence of Court of Session actions. These alternatives are dealt with below.

Originally, petitions for the recall of inhibitions proceeded as Inner House petitions. The present position (RC 189(a) (xv)) is that if the inhibition was originally granted by the bill procedure, the petition for recall goes to the Outer House. Consequently it would appear to follow that where (a) the inhibition was not granted by the bill procedure and (b) it is not recallable by motion or letter of application (see below), recall will be by Inner House petition. (It must be said that RC 190 sheds little light on the question.) If this is correct, certain types of case will go to the Inner House. For instance, suppose that an inhibition is granted on a warrant granted as part of the summons. Decree is granted, and the debt is thereupon paid. The inhibitor fails to grant a discharge. How is the debtor to have the inhibition recalled? Not by Outer House petition, since the inhibition was not granted by the bill procedure. Nor by motion, since the cause is no longer in dependence. An Inner House petition would therefore appear to be necessary.

Motion

Provided that three conditions are satisfied, recall can be by motion. These are: (a) the inhibition is on the dependence, and the cause is still depending; (b) it is a Court of Session cause; (c) the recall is at the instance of the defender rather than a third party. See RC 74(h). However, even where motion is possible, the practice has often been to proceed by petition. But in *Stuart v Stuart*[4] (1926) (an arrestment case) Lord Morrison disapproved of this practice save 'in very exceptional circumstances'.

Letter of application

The motion procedure is not available before the cause has called. Consequently where the cause has not called the procedure is by letter of application to the Deputy Principal Clerk of Session who will arrange a

3 1979 SLT (Notes) 89.
4 1926 SLT 31.

hearing before the Lord Ordinary. The details of this procedure are set forth in RC 74(g).

Recall where inhibition not yet recorded

It is competent to recall an inhibition even though it has not yet been recorded: *Dove v Henderson*[5] (1865). In that case there will be no entry in the Personal Register.

Interdict and caveat

It appears that it is competent to interdict a threatened inhibition, where it can be shown that an inhibition would be unjustified. Such interdict would have to be in the Court of Session, the Sheriff having no jurisdiction in inhibition. See *Beattie v Pratt*[6] (1880), and also pp 186–187 of *Burn-Murdoch on Interdict*. In *Craig v Anderson*[7] (1776) it was held incompetent to interdict the recording of an inhibition, but it may be doubted to what extent this decision would be followed in modern practice. On the question of whether it is possible to lodge a caveat against inhibition, there appears to be no authority. In the parallel case of arrestment it has recently been held in the Sheriff Court that a caveat is incompetent: *Wards v Kelvin Tank Services Ltd*[8] (1984). But that case was per incuriam, for the Sheriff was not referred to *Royal Bank of Scotland v Bank of Scotland*[9] (1729) where such a caveat was allowed by the Court of Session. John H. Sinclair at p 64 of his *Conveyancing Practice in Scotland* (1986) says that caveat is competent, but he does not cite authority.

Recording the recall

The only point to be noted under this head is that the decree or interlocutor of recall should not be recorded until the time for reclaiming has passed.

However, at this point there would appear to exist a procedural loophole, in that the applicant can obtain a CCI before the reclaiming days have passed. It is thought that the Keeper is under no duty to ascertain, before accepting the CCI for recording, that there has been

5 (1865) 3 M 339.
6 (1880) 7 R 1171.
7 (1776) 5 Broun Supp 482.
8 1984 SLT (Sh Ct) 39.
9 (1729) 1 Paton 14.

no reclaiming motion. It would thus in theory seem possible for there to appear in the Personal Register a CCI of recall even though there has been a successful reclaiming motion against the recall. The writer has, however, not heard that this has ever happened in practice.

Grounds for recall: inhibition in execution

In general the only ground on which an inhibition in execution will be recalled is that the debt has been paid. Where the debt has been paid the debtor should in the first instance apply to the inhibitor for a discharge. Recall will be appropriate only where the inhibitor has failed to grant a discharge. Procedure is by petition. Though the general rule is that this is the only ground for the recall of an inhibition in execution, there may be certain exceptions. Thus recall is, it seems, competent on the ground of procedural irregularity. For cases where the decree in favour of the inhibitor is attacked by suspension or reduction, see below. There is also the possibility that in some cases an inhibition may be partially recalled on the ground that it is 'ineffective'. See p 37, below.

Recall: document of debt

The grounds for recall of an inhibition on a document of debt would appear to be the same as for the recall of an inhibition on the dependence. Usually, though not invariably, inhibition on a document of debt is an inhibition in security, the debt not yet being due and resting owing, such as an inhibition against the acceptor of a bill of exchange laid on during the currency of the bill on the ground that the acceptor is vergens ad inopiam. In such a case the ground for recall will typically be that the special circumstances (such as vergens ad inopiam) which were alleged do not in fact prevail.

Recall: inhibition on the dependence

The extensive body of case law on the recall of inhibitions on the dependence does not easily lend itself to classification. But, speaking broadly, such an inhibition will be recalled (a) on payment, or (b) on caution or consignation, or (c) on evidence of nimiety or oppression, or (d) on proof of procedural irregularity. These will be considered in turn, except for the first, which seems too clear to require comment.

Caution or consignation

The debtor is always entitled to recall if he consigns the sum sued for or finds satisfactory caution for it. The reason is simply that such caution or consignation makes the diligence pointless and oppressive, since the pursuer is now secured for his claim. In practice caution or consignation leads to the extrajudicial discharge of the inhibition, but if the inhibitor is unco-operative, the defender can insist on recall. The Court is the judge of the amount to be consigned and of the sufficiency of the caution. (For the latter, see RC 238.) The Court is entitled to fix the sum to be consigned, or to be secured by caution, below the sum concluded for, and in practice in actions for damages where the sum correlated for is 'random' the Court will often fix a relatively low figure. Stewart at p 571 gives several nineteenth-century examples, and it is understood that modern practice is the same.

Oppression and nimiety

Whereas inhibition in execution is, generally speaking, a remedy to which the successful party has an absolute entitlement, inhibition on the dependence (and perhaps inhibition on a document of debt, at any rate where the debt is future or contingent) is essentially an equitable remedy. It will therefore be recalled if, in the judgment of the Court, its use, or its continued use, is inequitable. 'Nimiety' and 'oppression' are the terms used. There would seem to be no very clear distinction between them, and it is therefore convenient to treat them as denoting a single concept. By the very nature of the case it is not possible to give an exhaustive list of the circumstances which will, in the eyes of the Court, constitute nimiety or oppression. Each case will be judged only in the light of equity and the discretion of the Court applied. The following are illustrative examples.

(a) Where the inhibitor is already adequately secured for his claim. See Stewart, p 570. (Usually if a creditor is fully secured he will simply realise his security rather than sue, but this is not always easily done.)
(b) Where the debtor has heritable properties of such value that, given the sum sued for, there is no need for the inhibition to attach to all these properties. In such a case the recall ordered will be partial only. For an example see *McInally v Kildonan Homes Ltd*[10] (1979). (Such a recall necessarily involves some risk to the pursuer. Inhibition is only a freeze diligence and gives no real right, so however much the properties may be worth, the inhibitor may finally receive nothing.)
(c) Where arrestments on the dependence have given the pursuer adequate security. This proposition could be subsumed under either (a) or (b) above.

10 1979 SLT (Notes) 89.

(d) Where the financial standing of the debtor is such that it is unreasonable to say that the pursuer requires interim security. An illustration drawn from the law of arrestment is *Dundee Magistrates v Taylor*[11] (1863). It is suggested that in modern practice local authorities, state corporations, and the sort of commercial organisations whose shares would be reckoned as 'blue chips' could claim exemption from inhibition on the dependence on this principle.

(e) Where the debt is future or contingent, and special circumstances have not been pled. Alternatively, this might be classified as procedural irregularity (see below). See *Stevens v Campbell*[12] (1873), *Symington*[13] (1875). See also *Beton*[14] (1961).

(f) Where the debt is future or contingent, and though special circumstances have been averred, they are not substantiated. (For burden of proof, see p 37 below.)

Irregularity

Inhibition will be recalled on the ground of irregularity in its use. This applies, it appears, to inhibition in execution as well as to inhibition on the dependence and on a document of debt. Like other diligence, inhibition must be used stricti juris. There are numerous older cases in this area, heroically reviewed by Stewart at 541 to 546. See in particular *Walker v Hunter*[15] (1853). There is virtually no post-Stewart authority. In *Morton v Smith*[16] (1902) an inhibition was recalled since the purported service at the dwelling house was bad, the defender having at the date of service sailed for America with the purpose of emigration.

Further possibilities

Recall on caution or consignation, and recall on the ground of oppression or nimiety, are essentially the same, the principle being that the continued use of the inhibition would be inequitable. There are indications in the case law that this principle is capable of considerable extension. Thus in some cases it appears that the Court has recalled or restricted an inhibition on the ground that the pursuer's case was prima facie unlikely to succeed, or unlikely to succeed for the whole sum. This

11 (1863) 1 M 701.
12 (1873) 11 M 772.
13 (1875) 3 R 205.
14 1961 SLT (Notes) 19.
15 (1853) 16 D 226.
16 (1902) 9 SLT 396.

seems to have been the ratio of recall in *Turnbull's Trustee v Turnbulls*[17] (1823) and in *Hay v Morrison*[18] (1838) and possibly in *Beton v Beton*[19] (1961). And it seems to be some such interim assessment of probabilis causa which is the foundation of the practice of allowing caution or consignation of less than the sum sued for in reparation actions to warrant recall (see p 35, above).

Another possibility, though there is less authority for it, is that potential damage to the defender will be a consideration. Thus in *Barstow v Menzies*[20] (1840) the inhibition was recalled when the inhibitor failed to find caution for the potential loss to the defender. (See p 15 above.) This probably involves an interim assessment of the strength of the case, for if the inhibitor is eventually successful in his action, no question of damages will arise. It should be added that the possibilities discussed in this and the preceding paragraph do not concern inhibition in execution.

Burden of proof in recall

There seems to be little authority on the question of burden of proof in recall. It seems that the burden is on the party seeking recall. Except in the case of inhibition in execution, it may be questioned whether this rule is just.

Third party recall

Recall may be at the instance of a third-party, provided he can qualify title and interest, though this will be rare. An example: A inhibits B. B dispones to C. The debt to A is paid, but A does not discharge the inhibition. C may have the inhibition recalled. Procedure is by petition.

Recall or declarator on the ground of ineffectiveness

In certain types of case, an inhibition, though ineffective, nevertheless renders a property unmarketable because on the face of the registers it appears to be good. Two examples: (a) A is infeft but holds as nominee for B. A is inhibited, for his own debts. The inhibition is ineffective to prevent a disposition by A on the instructions of B, but in practice such a disposition will be stopped because a purchaser is unlikely to accept such

17 (1823) 2 S 459.
18 (1838) 16 S 1273.
19 1961 SLT (Notes) 19.
20 28 Jan 1840 Fac Dec.

a title. (b) C contracts to sell to D, and is thereafter inhibited. The inhibition is too late to stop the sale, but in practice D may decline to settle because the registers will show his (D's) infeftment to be later in date than the inhibition. (For further details, see chapters 6 and 12.) In cases of these types, the debtor will (failing a settlement with the inhibitor) wish to have the inhibition judicially found to be ineffective. This he is entitled to have done.

The obviously appropriate form of action is declarator. The decree will be recorded in the Personal Register. Is recall also competent? The advantage of recall is that in some cases it can be done much more quickly than declarator. These cases are those where the recall can proceed by motion or by letter of application rather than petition. It must be borne in mind that where recall/declarator is sought on the ground of ineffectiveness, time is often of the essence, for a purchaser is likely to resile if kept waiting.

The argument against the competency of recall is that nothing is being recalled. What is being obtained is simply a judicial asseveration of the actual subsisting effect of the inhibition, and this must therefore be by declarator. Whether this objection is well founded must await judicial decision. But it is understood that in practice inhibitions have been recalled on the ground of ineffectiveness. The only reported case appears to be *Beton v Beton*[1] (1961) where ineffectiveness was a ground on which recall was sought, though in the event recall was granted on another ground. (It should be observed that in this case as reported the argument of counsel appears to confuse ineffectiveness with incompetency. The two things are quite distinct: an ineffective inhibition is perfectly competent.)

In seeking recall or declarator on the ground of ineffectiveness, it is important to frame the motion or prayer or condescendence to make it clear that what is sought is a form of restriction rather than complete recall. Otherwise the application will be rejected for pluris petitio. Thus suppose that A concludes missives to sell to B, and is then inhibited. It would be wrong to recall the inhibition entirely, for A may have other property which ought to remain under the inhibition. Moreover, even to recall the inhibition over the property in question simpliciter would be wrong. After all, the sale to B might well fall through, and the inhibition is perfectly effective to bar any sale to any party other than B (or B's assignees). It is important therefore that the declarator or recall should be strictly limited in its terms. (In this connection note should be taken

1 1961 SLT (Notes) 19.

of the distinction between exempt property and exempt transactions. See chapter 4.)

It is sometimes supposed that recall, or partial recall, is necessary to enable an inhibited party to acquire property, or to grant a security over property to be acquired. This is not so, since inhibition does not affect acquirenda.

Expenses of recall

The question of the expenses of recall is not free from difficulty. There is a review of the question in *Laing v Muirhead*[2] (1868), but no decision was made. The matter is discussed by Stewart at p 573.

In the first place it is clear that in this area the law of inhibition and that of arrestment are largely the same.

Lord Justice Clerk Hope in *Clark v Loos*[3] (1855) says that 'the right to expenses in a recall of arrestments depends not upon the merits of the original action, but on the state of circumstances when the arrestments were used'. This is correct as a rule of thumb. The expenses of recall of diligence upon the dependence are in general independent of the outcome of the principal action. But it is thought that there are cases where the two are dealt with together.

The following propositions are suggested very tentatively as stating the modern law.

(1) When an inhibition on the dependence is recalled on the grounds of nimiety or oppression, the expenses fall against the inhibitor, regardless of the final outcome of the action. There is ample authority for this proposition. (See Stewart, p 573, and the authorities which he cites.)

(2) When an inhibition on the dependence is recalled on the ground of caution or consignation, then the law is unclear. Stewart (p 573) says that the expense falls on the debtor. But he does not cite authority for this statement. The case of *Blochairn v Flower*[4] (1865), it might be argued, supports Stewart's view. But there is some basis in the case law for saying that the correct practice is to reserve the question of expenses, until decree, and then to make the expenses follow the success of the action. Thus in *Dobbie v Duncanson*[5] (1872) Lord President Inglis says:

'The practice of this Division ... is, in recalling diligence on caution, to reserve expenses and to allow interim extract. That does

2 (1868) 6 M 282.
3 (1855) 17 D 306.
4 (1865) 1 SLR 45.
5 (1872) 10 M 810.

not preclude the petitioner, if he should be found right in the principal action, from coming back and asking to be found entitled to expenses.'

(The reference to interim extract assumes that the recall is by petition, as was the practice in 1872.) The writer inclines to the view that where inhibition on the dependence is recalled by reason of caution or consignation, the expenses of the recall will follow the success of the principal action.

(3) When an inhibition on the dependence has terminated in decree of dismissal or absolviter, or the action has been abandoned, the inhibitor comes under an obligation to grant a discharge, at his own expense. If he fails to do so then the inhibition may be recalled and the whole expenses will fall on the inhibitor. See *White v Ballantyne*[6] (1824, *Jack v Dalrymple*[7] (1828), *Sheriff v Balmer*[8] (1842), *Milne v Birrell*[9] (1902).

(4) When there is an inhibition in execution, or an inhibition on the dependence has been followed by decree for the pursuer, and the sum sued for is paid, it would seem that once more the inhibitor comes under an obligation to grant a discharge, but this time the discharge must be at the expense of the debtor. If however the inhibitor fails to grant such a discharge, a petition for recall will be necessary, and the expenses of such a petition will, it is thought, go against the inhibitor.

(5) When there is an inhibition on the dependence, and the claim is settled, then the inhibitor comes under an obligation to grant an extrajudicial discharge. The expense of the discharge should be one of the points decided in the settlement. If he fails to grant the discharge, the debtor may have the inhibition judicially recalled, and the inhibitor will be liable for the expenses. See *Robertson v Park Dobson*[10] (1896).

(6) There is authority (*Lickley, Petitioner*[11] (1871)), with which Stewart (p 573) agrees, to the effect that if an inhibitor refuses to grant a discharge when under an obligation to do so, and a petition for recall is made, the petitioner can then refuse any subsequent offer to discharge, and insist on his petition, and obtain expenses.

6 (1824) 2 S 770.
7 (1828) 7 S 219.
8 (1842) 4 D 453.
9 (1902) 4 F 879.
10 (1896) 24 R 30.
11 (1871) 8 SLR 624.

(7) If an inhibitor is under an obligation to grant a discharge, and the debtor raises a petition for recall without having first asked for such a discharge, the petition, though competent, must be at the expense of the debtor, since he has chosen the more expensive route. See *Gordon v Duncan*[12] (1827).

(8) When an inhibition is recalled on the ground of procedural irregularity, it seems clear, on general principles, that the expenses go against the inhibitor, regardless of the outcome of the principal action.

(9) When an inhibition is for a future or contingent debt, and it emerges that there exist no 'special circumstances' to justify its use, the question as to the expenses of recall is unclear. Stewart appears not to deal with it. In *Symington*[13] (1875) expenses were awarded against the debtor, but only on the principle that he was the husband, and that husbands are liable for the expenses of consistorial causes. The general principle should be that the expenses of recall should fall on the inhibitor, since the inhibition is unlawful. In effect this is simply a case of irregularity.

(10) The expenses of an unsuccessful application for recall would seem to go against the applicant. See *Muir v United Collieries*[14] (1908).

(11) When the inhibition is recalled by petition, the decree must either award expenses or reserve the question. If it does neither, then each party must meet his own expenses. See Stewart, p 573, and *Dobbie v Duncanson*[15] (1872). This point cannot arise when the recall is by motion.

(12) Apart from the last point, there would seem to be no difference in this area between petition and motion.

(13) Authority seems to be lacking as to who must pay for the fee for registering the recall in the Personal Register. Stewart (p 573) says that the expense always falls on the debtor, but as far as the writer can see the case which he cites does not support the proposition. The sensible approach would perhaps be to say that the fee must be paid by the inhibitor if the inhibition is recalled on the ground of nimiety or oppression, or irregularity, or lapse, or abandonment, but otherwise by the debtor.

---

12 (1827) 5 S 602.
13 (1875) 3 R 205.
14 1908 SC 768.
15 (1872) 10 M 810.

Lapse

'The effect of inhibition on a depending action rests entirely on the decree. If the action shall not terminate in a decree, the inhibition has no effect.' (Bell, 1.138.) A decree of dismissal or of absolvitor has the effect of terminating any inhibition used by the pursuer on the dependence of the action. There is no technical term to denominate this form of extinction: it is suggested that the term 'lapse' may conveniently be adopted. When Bell speaks of the action not resulting in a decree, he means a decree for the inhibitor. Nor must the passage quoted be taken to mean that an inhibition lapses merely as a result of the action falling asleep. An inhibition remains in force notwithstanding that the action has fallen asleep.

Where an inhibition is extinguished by lapse, the inhibitor thereby comes under an obligation to grant a discharge. He must meet his own expense in doing so. It does not seem to have been decided whether the defender can also insist on being paid his own law agent's fee for drafting the discharge, and the recording fee, but on the principle of the decisions cited in the previous pages, it would seem that he is so entitled. If the inhibitor fails to grant the discharge, the defender is entitled to judicial recall. Procedure is by petition. The expenses of the recall will be awarded against the inhibitor, since the petition was rendered necessary as a result of his wrongful refusal to grant a discharge.

As an alternative to discharge or recall, the defender can register the decree of dismissal or absolvitor in the Personal Register. The extract is required, not just a copy. But the defender is under no obligation to adopt this procedure. He is entitled to insist on a discharge which failing a recall. See the cases cited above.

Indeed, it is preferable for the Register to be cleared by discharge or recall. The reason is that a discharge or recall will specify the inhibition in question. An extract decree of absolvitor or dismissal will not do so, which leads to the unsatisfactory result that the extinction is a matter of interference rather than direct inspection.

Reduction and suspension

The reduction of a decree on which inhibition has been used extinguishes the inhibition. While it may be competent to extract the decree of reduction and record it, the normal procedure is as in a decree of absolvitor. That is to say, the inhibitor is bound to grant a discharge, which failing recall will be granted. The most convenient approach would perhaps be to insert conclusions for such recall in the action of reduction.

A careful distinction must be made (though it is often not made) between suspension of a charge and suspension of a decree. The former has, by definition, no effect on diligences other than poinding. However, in many cases the reasons which underlie the suspension of the charge may also constitute good grounds for applying for the recall of other diligence used, such as inhibition.

A suspension of a decree may be either interim or final. Interim suspension has no effect on any inhibition used on the decree, but nevertheless the grounds of the interim suspension may in practice afford grounds for a recall. This, however, will normally proceed as a separate process. See *Matheson v Simpson*[16] (1822). A final suspension of a decree has the effect of a reduction, for which see above.

Death

An inhibition is unaffected by the death of the inhibitor. The effect of the death of the debtor is not so free from doubt. The older authorities are clear that an inhibition has no effect against the heir of the deceased debtor. (See Stewart, p 554.) But they are silent on the following two cases: (a) where the debtor makes a mortis causa disposal of his heritage, and (b) where the debtor has made an inter vivos disposal which is not yet complete at the date of death (typically where missives have been concluded but the transaction has not yet settled).

The position is further complicated by the fact that since the Succession (Scotland) Act 1964 the succession of the heir of line has been abolished and heritage now falls under executry.

As a result it is difficult to state the current law with any certainty. At one extreme the doctrine that the executor is eadem persona cum defuncto might be founded on to argue that the executor is affected by the inhibition, and consequently that any disposal (whether by the docket procedure or otherwise) by him (and whether or not in implement of the will, if any) will be reducible by the inhibitor. The author would be reluctant to accept this argument because he suspects that the eadem persona doctrine, though always honoured with lip-service, is of doubtful standing. It is suggested that our law ascribes to the executor a legal personality distinct from that of the defunct except for certain limited purposes. The point, however, cannot be gone into in a work of this nature.

Another conceivable position would be to say that the executor is barred by the inhibition from implementing the mortis causa disposals, since they are voluntary disposals on the part of the inhibited party, but that the executor is nevertheless free to make any other transfer of the heritage. On this view, then, inhibition would, roughly speaking, strike

16 (1822) 1 S 542.

at a testate estate, but not at an intestate one. This position possesses a certain abstract cogency, but produces a result which, to the author at least, seems absurd.

A third position would be to say that an inhibition is extinguished by the debtor's death, so that the executor is free to dispose of the heritage. Thus Walter Ross writes that 'inhibition, being only personal to the debtor, falls at his decease' (*Lectures*, vol. p 497 of 1822 edition). A modern argument in support of this position would be that the executor takes title through confirmation. Confirmation is a judicial conveyance. Being judicial, it is involuntary on the part of the deceased. Since the confirmation is a transfer of the heritage which cannot be reduced by the inhibitor, the executor's title cannot be challenged, and those taking title through the executor have the same protection.

Whilst the author sees no conclusive reason for preferring any of these positions over the others, he would favour the third, as being more in harmony with the older authorities, and also cogent in itself.

It is sometimes competent for the executor to deduce title through the will without confirmation (see (1965) 10 JLSS 153), though this is not now common. In such a case, it is uncertain whether the inhibition against the deceased would be of any effect. It is thought that it would not.

Similar difficulties beset the situation where the debtor has made an inter vivos disposal not completed at the date of death. The author is unable to offer even a tentative solution to this conundrum.

For the question of inhibition against the executor himself, see chapter 2.

Prescription

Inhibition prescribes after five years: s 44 of the 1924 Act, replacing s 42 of the Conveyancing (Scotland) Act 1874, which was to the same effect. The quinquennium begins to run on the day when the inhibition takes effect. This is the day when it is recorded in the Personal Register. But if the Notice procedure has been adopted, and the inhibition has been recorded within 21 days of the Notice, then prescription will run from the date of the Notice.

The rule is the same irrespective of whether the inhibition is in execution or on the dependence or on a document of debt. The point is worth stressing since in the law of arrestment an arrestment in execution prescribes from its date whereas an arrestment on the dependence prescribes not from its date but from the date of the decree (Personal Diligence Act 1838, s 22). Thus to give a concrete example, if an inhibition on the dependence is recorded on 1 March and decree in favour of the inhibitor is pronounced on 1 October, the inhibition will prescribe five years after 1 March and not five years after 1 October.

Section 42 of the Conveyancing (Scotland) Act 1874 allowed the inhibition to be saved from prescription by the recording of an appropriate memorandum within the five year period. This was called renewing the inhibition. This procedure was abolished by s 44(6) of the 1924 Act. Although it is no longer competent to renew an inhibition, there is nothing to stop the creditor from re-inhibiting. The difference between the two is procedural. Renewal of an inhibition involved simply making the appropriate entry in the Personal Register. Re-inhibition involves going back to square one, obtaining warrant to inhibit and so forth. There may possibly be also a difference in effect between renewal and re-inhibition. This will be discussed below.

Effect of extinction

Extinction, in the first place, means that all future debts and deeds by the inhibited party are free from the inhibition. So much is clear. What is less clear is whether the extinction is to be considered as operating retro so as to validate violations (if any) made while the inhibition was in effect. This question is one of some importance, but curiously not only is there no authority but also there appears to be virtually no discussion of the question in the literature. What follows therefore is necessarily speculative.

It is clear that when an inhibition on the dependence lapses by the failure of the action it is extinguished for all purposes, so that any violations cease to be challengeable.

The case of recall is not quite so clear, but it seems reasonable to take the same view. If it is just that the inhibition be recalled on the ground of caution or consignation, or nimiety and oppression, then it also seems just that the recall should operate ab initio, since whatever justification there was for the inhibition has now either been removed (caution or consignation) or shown to be unfounded (nimiety and oppression).

In the case of discharge by payment, the same rule must apply. The inhibitor can have no interest in challenging earlier violations. In certain cases a discharge will be granted voluntarily without payment. In such cases it is presumably open to the granter to reserve to himself the right to challenge earlier debts and deeds, ie to restrict the effect of the discharge to future acts. But if no such restriction appears in the discharge it is thought that the presumption must be that the discharge is to operate retro.

In all the cases so far considered the event which operates extinction also operates, so to speak, to remove the ground of the inhibition. Rather different are the two other cases, namely death and prescription. In the case of death it seems fairly clear that it would be inequitable to allow the death to validate retrospectively violations of the inhibition done while the inhibited party was alive. (The case of *Roberts v Potter & Reid*[17] (1829) is not contrary to the view here expressed.)

More difficult is the case of prescription. Let A inhibit B in year 1. In year 6, one week before the expiry of the inhibition, B grants a standard security to C. Does A's right to reduce this vanish at the end of the week? Or will the right to reduce continue thereafter?

At common law the rule was that an inhibition never did prescribe. It continued indefinitely till extinguished by some other means. But if some deed by the debtor violated the inhibition the right to reduce the transaction was liable to prescribe. It would be cut off by the long negative prescription, then 40 years. (See eg Bankton, 1.7.143; *Duff's Feudal Conveyancing*, p 183.) This indefinite continuance of an inhibition was felt to be unsatisfactory by the Bell Commission, the great nineteenth-century commission whose recommendations, contained in three Reports, were gradually implemented in a series of statutes. The matter is dealt with at pp 19, 20 and 30 of the Second Report of 1835, the recommendation being that 'inhibition shall be limited in its effect to five years'. Unfortunately the question of whether the expiry of the five years should operate retro so as to validate prior breaches was not considered by them. When this particular recommendation was implemented, by s 42 of the Conveyancing (Scotland) Act 1874, the point was again ignored, the section simply saying that inhibitions 'shall prescribe on the lapse of five years'. This is ambiguous. It would be pointless to ask what was the intention of Parliament, since it seems that the ambiguity had struck no one, for otherwise the draftsmen would have made the point clear. Section 42 of the 1874 Act was later repealed and replaced by s 44 of the Conveyancing (Scotland) Act 1924, which provides that inhibitions 'shall prescribe and be of no effect on the lapse of five years'.

In the period 1874–1924 the question was of little importance, since the inhibitor could protect his inhibition from prescription by renewal under s 42 of the Conveyancing (Scotland) Act 1874. But since 1924 renewal has not been competent. Re-inhibition is competent, but if the view is taken that prescription operates retroactive validation, a re-inhibition may be useless. Thus in year 1, A inhibits B. In year 4, B dispones to C. In year 5, A re-inhibits B. This is a separate inhibition from the first inhibition, and can have no bearing on whether and when the right to reduce the disposition to C prescribes. (See further John Burns, *Conveyancing Guide* (1924), p 80.)

17 (1829) 7 S 611.

Three arguments tend to point to the conclusion that the right to reduce a violation does not prescribe at the same time as the inhibition itself. The first is that the object of the recommendation in the Bell Report seems to have been simply to remove the evil of the imprescriptibility of inhibition. The right to reduce was already prescriptible. The second argument is that the language of s 44 of the 1924 Act, like that of s 42 of the Conveyancing (Scotland) Act 1874, is silent as to the prescription of the right to reduce. It speaks only of the prescription of the inhibition itself. The third argument is that if the right to reduce prescribes with the inhibition itself, the strange result is that a violation in the first years of the inhibition will prescribe in about four years, while a violation in the last week of the inhibition will prescribe in a matter of days.

Against these arguments is the fact that Stewart assumed that the effect of s 42 of the act of 1874 was that the right to reduce prescribed simultaneously with the inhibition itself. (Stewart, p 575.) However, his authority on this point is lessened by the fact that he does not analyse the problem.

At first sight it might seem that the problem can be solved by appealing to conveyancing practice. The practice of conveyancers is to make a personal search for no more than five years back from the date of the transaction. This might be taken to mean that conveyancers assume that links in the title more than five years old (but still within the positive prescription) which violated some inhibition, have become unchallengeable. But the regrettable truth is that it is possible to draw no conclusion from conveyancing practice. For a five year search is, strictly speaking, insufficient on *either* theory. For even if we say (with Stewart) that the right to reduce expires with the inhibition itself, it may still be the case that the inhibitor has in fact within the quinquennium raised the necessary action. This does, of course, not stop the inhibition from prescribing, but it does keep alive his rights as against the particular violation. Thus on any view it is always possible that a link in title more than five years old is still voidable on the ground of an inhibition recorded more than five years ago. Consequently the conveyancing practice of searching back only five years seems to support neither the one theory nor the other.

The question of whether the right to reduce breaches prescribes simultaneously with the inhibition itself appears therefore not to be capable of definite answer.

It remains only to add that if the position is taken that the right to reduce does not prescribe with the inhibition itself, then the common law rule continues in force, namely that the right to reduce is eventually cut off by the long negative prescription, which of course is currently 20 years. The relevant statutory provision is probably s 8 rather than s 7 of the Prescription and Limitation of Actions (Scotland) Act 1973. Alternatively (and this may be the better view) the right of reduction may be cut off by positive prescription after ten years, under s 1 of the Act.

Since the above was written, an article by D. J. Cusine has appeared in (1987) 32 JLSS (February) arguing along similar lines.

Damages for wrongous use

As with other diligences, the wrongous use of inhibition is a delict which will give the inhibited party a claim for damages. To qualify as wrongous it is not enough that the claim should in fact be unfounded. It is necessary that the inhibition should have been used with malice and without probable cause. (Stewart, p 773.) The question is most likely to come up in connection with inhibition on the dependence, but an inhibition in execution might also be actionable, eg where a pursuer inhibited after receiving full payment. Actions for wrongous inhibition seem to be rare in practice.

CHAPTER 4

Property

Scope of chapter

Inhibition strikes at certain debts and deeds which affect or may affect the heritable estate of the debtor. This chapter considers precisely what property is so affected. Subsquent chapters will consider what deeds and debts are struck at, and what the consequences of contraventions are.

Heritable property

Inhibition is a diligence against the heritable estate of the debtor. Thus the statutory style for letters of inhibition (1868 Act, Schedule QQ) provides that the debtor is inhibited from 'selling, disponing, conveying, burdening or otherwise affecting his lands or heritages to the prejudice of the complainer'.

How the line is to be drawn between heritable and moveable is a question for the law of property. But three points are worth stressing here. (a) Rights may be heritable, and so affectable by inhibition, notwithstanding that they are incorporeal. Thus a lease, which is incorporeal heritable estate in the hands of the lessee, is affectable by an inhibition by the lessee's creditor. Or again, a heritable security is incorporeal heritable estate in the hands of the heritable creditor, and so is affectable by inhibition by the creditors of the heritable creditor. (b) A right may be heritable, and so affectable by inhibition, even though there has been no completion of title. Thus where there has been a security by way of ex facie absolute disposition, the debtor is uninfeft, but his right is heritable and thus subject to inhibition. (See eg *George M. Allen Ltd v Waugh's Trustee*[1] (1966). (c) A right may be heritable (or moveable) in itself while being deemed moveable (or heritable) for some particular purposes, such as the law of succession. A well-known example is s 117 of the 1868 Act, whereby heritable securities are made partially moveable in the succession of a deceased heritable creditor, while remaining heritable in themselves. (Hence it is that a creditor of

1 1966 SLT (Sh Ct) 17.

the heritable creditor will proceed against the security by way of inhibition and adjudication and not by way of arrestment.) See further Bell, 2,135 and Stewart, p 547.

Is the right of a purchaser under missives heritable or moveable? In *Leeds Permanent Building Society v Aitken Malone and Mackay*[2] (1986) it was held that such a right is moveable, and that the right of the purchaser does not become heritable until the disposition has been delivered to him. The writer respectfully suggests that there must be some doubt as to whether this decision is correct. A full discussion of this case would be out of place in a work of this nature, since the issue is essentially one of property law. It is for property law to classify rights as heritable or moveable, and for the law of diligence to apply those classifications. But the writer would observe that it is settled law that the right of a purchaser under missives is heritable in succession (though the authorities on this point do not seem to have been cited in the case itself). This is of course not conclusive (see the last paragraph) but it is respectfully suggested that it does at least raise a presumption that the right is heritable in itself.

If correct, the decision also leads to the strange result that once missives have been concluded, it will be beyond the reach of inhibition by creditors of *either* party. (A somewhat similar criticism of the decision has been made by John H. Sinclair at the PQLE course on conveyancing, December 1986. See pp 11–12 of the conference papers.)

It should be noted that the decision, if correct, leads to the result that a party who holds heritable property on missives is free to sell such property in disregard of any inhibition against him. This result is contrary to the traditional understanding of conveyancers.

The implications of the *Leeds* case will be further considered later in this chapter and also in chapters 12 and 13.

The adjudgeability requirement

In general all heritable rights are affectable by inhibition. But this rule is subject to the qualification that only adjudgeable rights can be affected by inhibition. Thus Bell (2,135): 'It is established that an inhibition is effectual to secure those subjects only which are affectable by adjudication.' Since as a general rule, all rights which are heritable are adjudgeable, this qualification is normally an unimportant one. Its main practical importance tends to arise in connection with leases.

2 1986 SLT 338.

Leases

This section deals with inhibition against a lessee. For inhibition against a lessor, see chapter 6.

A lease is a heritable incorporeal right and thus potentially subject to inhibition. Whether, in any particular case, it is actually so subject depends upon the destination in the lease. The reason for this is that the adjudgeability of a lease depends on its destination, and, as was explained above, inhibition is effectual only as against adjudgeable subjects.

A lease may be freely assignable either by reason of an express destination to that effect or by implication of the law where there is no destination. (In the absence of an express destination the law will make some leases assignable and some not so. For further details see the standard texts on the law of leases.) If it is freely assignable then it is adjudgeable by the creditors of the lessee. In this context an adjudger is regarded as a species of assignee. (See eg Stewart, p 601.)

The case is different where the lease is not freely assignable. Non-assignability may be as a result of an express destination to that effect, or, in the absence of a destination, by operation of law. If a lease is non-assignable it cannot be adjudged and therefore cannot be affected by inhibition. See Stewart, p 601, *Elliot v Duke of Buccleugh*[3] (1747), and *Cunningham v Hamilton*[4] (1770).

Normally the question of the effect of inhibition on a non-assignable lease will not arise, for there will be no assignation of it for the inhibitor to object to. But sometimes such a lease is assigned with the consent of the landlord. Such an assignation will be unaffected by any inhibition against the cedent.

The same rules apply to renunciations of leases, since renunciation is in effect but an assignation to the landlord. Thus *Paton & Cameron on Landlord and Tenant* (1967), p 59: 'If a lease excludes assignees and subtenants, and inhibition does not prevent the tenant from renouncing it in favour of the landlord.' The leading case in this context is *Fraser v Marquess of Abercorn*[5] (1835) where this was one of the rationes for refusing reduction by the inhibitor. (It is to be noted in referring to this case that although the inhibition was registered after the date of the renunciation, it was possible under the old law for an inhibition to come into operation up to 60 days before registration.)

3 (1747) Mor 10329.
4 (1770) Mor 10410.
5 (1835) 14 S 77.

It would be fairly plain sailing if all destinations in leases were clearly the one thing or the other. But very often destinations occupy a half-way house between assignability and non-assignability. One style which can be quickly dealt with is the destination which forbids assignation except with the consent of the landlord. It is now quite settled that such a destination is no different in effect from one which prohibits assignation simpliciter. (See eg *Paton & Cameron on Landlord and Tenant* (1967), p 153.) More problematic is the destination, often seen in commercial leases, which adds the proviso 'which consent shall not be unreasonably withheld' or similar words. This is a clause borrowed from English law, where it has a settled interpretation. There seems to be no Scottish authority. The only Scottish material on it is the article by Phillips at (1976) 21 JLSS 436. Though this is an excellent article, Phillips does discuss whether such a destination would exclude an adjudger (and hence make inhibition inoperative). In this area only guesses are possible, but the guess of the author would be that such a lease is adjudgeable (provided that the adjudger would be a person acceptable to the reasonable landlord, and so on, along the lines of English law). Hence such a lease would be affected by inhibition. But it must be stressed that these are no more than guesses.

Another clause sometimes seen in commercial leases is the right to assign to a subsidiary or parent company or to another company in the same group. In that case it is thought that an assignation to such an associated company would not be struck at unless there were in the destination other more general assignability provisions. But again this is only a guess.

It is thought that inhibition will strike at subletting where there is power to sublet. Subletting bears to assignation essentially the same relation as feuing does to disponing.

In general a standard security over a registered lease will be struck at by a prior inhibition.

Inhibition against a lessee will not stop the landlord from irritating the lease. This is because the forfeiture by the lessee is not a 'voluntary' act in the relevant sense.

Matrimonial occupancy rights

There can be no question that the occupancy rights conferred by the Matrimonial Homes (Family Protection) (Scotland) Act 1981 are not affectable by inhibition. If for no other reason, this is because, being personal to the holder, they could not be adjudged.

Acquisata and acquirenda

At common law it made no difference when the debtor acquired the property. The inhibition affected property acquired after its date (acquirenda) just as much as property already held (acquisata). This rule was altered by s 157 of the Act of 1868: 'No inhibition . . . shall have any force or effect as against any lands to be acquired' after the date on which the inhibition comes into effect. The word 'lands' is defined in s 3 of the Act as including 'all heritable subjects, securities and rights'. The former section has a proviso preserving the common law where the debtor is, at the date of the inhibition, the successor to property 'by deed of entail or by a similar indefeasible title'. The precise meaning of this proviso will not be discussed since it is of little importance in modern law. Burns gives his views at p 298. But it is worth signposting one pitfall: a destination is not 'indefeasible' within the meaning of the proviso merely because it is non-evacuable (eg within the rule of *Perrett's Trs v Perrett*[6] (1909)), since such a destination remains capable of being defeated by inter vivos disposal. (See eg *Steele v Caldwell*[7] (1979).)

In the usual case the acquisition of heritable property involves three stages: (1) conclusion of missives; (2) delivery of the disposition; (3) infeftment. It is only at the third stage that the purchaser acquires the real right of ownership. Clearly, once this third stage is reached, the property is acquisata from the point of view of the law of inhibition. But what of the prior stages?

In *Leeds Permanent Building Society v Aitken Malone and Mackay*[8] (1986) it was held that the purchaser's right becomes acquisata at stage (2), ie at the delivery of the disposition, rather than at stage (1) or (3). This may be correct, but mentioned earlier in this chapter the basis for the decision may be questioned. Traditional conveyancing practice has been (eg in the context of searches) that property is acquisata for the purposes of inhibition as soon as missives have been concluded (stage (1)). In chapter 12 it is suggested that notwithstanding the *Leeds* case the safe course is to adhere to the traditional practice.

For completeness it must be added that there is obviously at least a stateable case for saying that property is not acquisata for the purposes of the law of inhibition until stage (3) has been reached.

The writer is unable to come to a definite conclusion as to the stage at which property becomes acquisata. Perhaps the most logical position would be that inhibition does strike at a purchaser's right under missives, but that the inhibition will then cease to have effect upon delivery of the disposition since such delivery supersedes missives. But while the writer takes up no position on this matter, he would, as stated above, recommend that in conveyancing practice the traditional safety-first approach should be continued.

6 1909 SC 522.
7 1979 SLT 228.
8 1986 SLT 338.

Trust property

Consideration is given to trusts in chapter 5. In brief, a trustee may be inhibited for a trust debt. This will affect the trust estate but not the trustee's private estate. Conversely an inhibition against a person as an individual has no effect against property held by him as a trustee. Inhibition against a beneficiary is effectual to the extent that the interest of the beneficiary falls to be classified as heritable.

Executry estate

Executry being a species of trust, broadly the same rules apply as for trusts generally. It appears that an inhibition against the defunct does not effect the executor. See p 43.

Trusts and acquirenda

Whether a beneficial interest in a trust is acquisata or acquirenda depends on vesting. If the interest has vested at the date of the inhibition, it is acquisata, and if not, not. Thus suppose that trustees hold in trust for A in liferent and for B whom failing C in fee, there is (as is well known) no vesting of the beneficial fee so long as all three parties are alive. Consequently an inhibition against B while A and C are alive would be of no effect.

Latent trusts

It sometimes happens that property is held under a latent trust, ie the trustee appears from the face of the titles to be the absolute owner. This is particularly common in 'nominee' trusts, ie where A holds property as nominee for B. In such a case it is thought that a third party taking a title from the nominee will be affected by an inhibition against the party beneficially entitled (here B) if but only if the third party knew or ought to have known the identity the party so beneficially entitled. A third party acting in complete good faith cannot be penalised.

Joint and common property

The distinction between joint and common property is well known and will not be discussed here. (See K. G. C. Reid at 1985 SLT (News) 57.) For practical purposes the main example of joint ownership of heritage is trust property, owned jointly by all the trustees, for which see above. In the case of common ownership (such as husband and wife owning the matrimonial home in 'joint names' ie not jointly but in common) the problem is what is the effect of an inhibition against just one of the common owners. The nature of common property is that each owner has a share which he can sell or otherwise deal with independently of the co-owner(s). It follows therefore that if he is inhibited he will be barred from selling his share or otherwise affecting it. In other words the speciality that the debtor's interest happens to be common property is irrelevant. Though there is no authority on this point, it is submitted that there can be no doubt that the law is as stated.

What is the effect on the other co-owner(s)? Although the other co-owner's share is, of course, unaffected by the inhibition, the inhibition will mean that the property cannot be sold as a whole. (This is on the supposition that a right in common can be adjudged. See chapter 13.) Although in theory he could sell his own share separately, in practice this is seldom feasible. The general rule of common property is that *nemo in communione invite detineri potest*, so that one co-owner can, if necessary, apply to the Court for an equitable division of the subjects, or (as is much more common) for the sale of the property as a whole and the division of the proceeds. Although authority is lacking, it is submitted that it is clear that an inhibition against one co-owner cannot deprive the other co-owner of his right to take such action. In such a case, the purchaser could not object to the title offered. The reason for this is that inhibition strikes only at voluntary acts, and a sale at the direction of the Court at the instance of the non-inhibited co-owner would not be in the relevant sense a voluntary act. (For such a result, it is of course requisite that the sale should proceed by the authority of the Court. The inhibited party could not consent to a voluntary sale.)

If such a sale takes place the position of the inhibitor will be essentially the same as of an inhibitor who finds that the subjects are sold by a heritable creditor. (See chapter 9.)

In the event that the Court orders not sale but an equitable physical division it is thought that the inhibition will continue in effect as against the portion of the subjects allotted to the debtor.

There is no authority on the question of whether it would be contemplated for the inhibited party to apply to the Court for a division or a sale and division, and the general principles of the law of inhibition do not readily suggest a solution.

Exempt property and exempt transactions

It is necessary to distinguish between exempt property and exempt transactions. Exempt property is property (such as acquirenda) which is not affected by a given inhibition. An exempt transaction is a transaction which relates to non-exempt property but which is itself exempt from the operation of the inhibition. As an illustration of this distinction, suppose that on 1 May A borrows money from B and obliges himself to grant in security of the loan a standard security over certain property. He duly delivers the standard security on 30 May. Meanwhile, on 15 May, he is inhibited. Now, the granting of the standard security is an exempt transaction, since it was already contracted at the date of the inhibition, inhibition striking only at future voluntary acts. But the property itself is not exempt property. Thus if A sought to grant a second standard security over that property to another party, he would find that the inhibition prevented him from doing so.

Property outwith Scotland

Inhibition affects only immoveable property situated in Scotland. The inhibited debtor remains free to dispose of his immoveable estate outwith Scotland. If the inhibitor wishes to take steps against such property he must do so in accordance with the law of the jurisdiction where the property is situated.

Foreign debtors

The corollary of the last paragraph is that inhibition affects property notwithstanding that its proprietor may be a national of, or domiciled in, a place outwith Scotland. The reason for this, and for the last paragraph, is that the general rule of international private law is that diligence is governed by the law of the situs of the assets. Some further consideration of inhibition against foreign debtors is given in the next chapter.

CHAPTER 5

Parties

Scope of chapter

This chapter considers inhibition in relation to special parties, ie parties other than the ordinary case of an individual person. To a considerable extent the question of special parties is considered in other chapters in connection with particular topics, so several of the headings below will merely summarise the law and give a cross-reference. This chapter also looks at the effect on inhibition of foreign administrative proceedings.

The Crown

Though express authority is lacking, there can be no doubt that inhibition against the Crown is incompetent. As creditor, the Crown may inhibit (and often does so, especially in connection with the recovery of taxes). Such inhibition is subject to the ordinary law of inhibition and has no special privileges (cf s 26 of the Crown Proceedings Act 1947, and also Stewart, p 546). If the Crown is a party affected by the inhibition at the instance of another inhibitor, eg is the grantee of a disposition in contravention of an inhibition, there can be no question but that the inhibition is effectual as against the Crown. Thus in the case mentioned the inhibitor could reduce and adjudge.

Corporations

No specialities apply to bodies corporate with respect to inhibitions, except as to the procedures of liquidation, receivership and administration, for which see chapter 11.

Partnerships

Heritable property held on feudal title is taken in the name of one or more of the partners as trustees for the firm. The inhibition, however, is against the firm itself (being a separate person in the eyes of the law) rather than against such partners as happen to be trustees. But warrant to inhibit the firm is also considered as warrant to inhibit the partners as individuals. (*Ewing v McClelland*[1] (1860).) Such inhibition will then operate against the private heritable estate of the partners. If, however, the inhibition is only against the firm, it will not affect the private estates of the partners.

Trustees

A trustee may be effectually inhibited in respect of a trust debt. It must design him in his capacity as trustee, or it will be bad. On the general law of diligence, such an inhibition will be of no effect as against his private estate. Conversely, an inhibition against the trustee for a private debt will affect only his private estate and will have no effect against heritage held by him in trust. In the case of an ordinary inter vivos trust, if the truster was inhibited when he set up the trust, the inhibition will be effective against the conveyance to the trustee in relation to the heritable estate. For insolvency trustees, see below.

Beneficiaries

The interest of a beneficiary in a trust will be affectable by inhibition against that beneficiary if his interest is itself heritable, but not otherwise. The typical instance of this is where the beneficiary has a vested right to an identifiable heritable property. For instance, if trustees hold heritage in liferent for A and in fee for B, and B is inhibited, the inhibition is good. It need hardly be said that what is affected by the inhibition is not the title vested in the trustee, but merely the beneficiary's interest therein. Thus the inhibition will not stop the trustees from conveying to the beneficiary. The same holds good for legatees, since legatees are simply a species of beneficiary. See further *McLaren on Wills and Succession* (3rd edn), para 1567, 1568, and *Wilson and Duncan on Trusts* (1975), p 128.

Parties outwith Scotland

There are no specialities which apply to parties outwith Scotland, such as foreign corporations, owning heritable property within Scotland. Inhibition has no effect as against immoveable property situated furth of Scotland. For foreign liquidators etc, see below.

Joint and common owners

The only significant class of joint owners are trustees, as above. Other cases where heritable property is vested in more than one person will normally be cases of ownership in common, such as where a husband

---

1 (1860) 22 D 1347.

and wife take title in 'joint' names, ie in common. In such a case an inhibition against one of the co-owners will be effective as against his share, but cannot prejudice the position of the other co-owner. The matter is more fully discussed in chapter 4. (This is on the supposition that rights in common can be adjudged. See chapter 13.)

Occupancy rights

A spouse who has no ownership of the matrimonial home may neverthe-less have 'occupancy rights' under the Matrimonial Homes (Family Protection) (Scotland) Act 1981. An inhibition against such a spouse (the 'non-entitled spouse') has no effect in relation to such occupancy rights. Thus in particular it cannot prevent that spouse from renouncing those rights or from consenting to a 'dealing'. The reason is that occupancy rights are non-adjudgeable and therefore cannot be affected by inhibition. (See further chapter 4.)

Representative parties

The most difficult questions tend to arise in connection with those who may loosely be described as representative parties, such as executors, liquidators, judicial factors and so on. The law in such cases is not always certain. In all such cases the question arises in a double manner, firstly in relation to an inhibition against the party who is represented (eg against a company before it is wound up) and secondly in relation to the representative party (eg the liquidator). The very tentative view of the writer is that if the representative has been judicially constituted as such (eg an executor by his confirmation, a trustee in sequestration by his act and warrant, and so forth) then he takes free form the inhibition in this sense, that he may sell or otherwise deal with the heritable subjects without such dealings being reducible. On the other hand the inhibition may still be effectual to give the inhibitor a preference upon the proceeds of sale in competition with post-inhibition creditors, if any. These rules, it is further submitted, may apply to representative parties who though not judicially constituted, are in a similar position, such as liquidators acting in voluntary liquidations. The position of a trustee acting under a voluntary trust deed for behoof of creditors presents special problems. Where the representative party is in fact merely acting to enforce a security right (such as a heritable creditor or a receiver) it is submitted that he can sell the subjects free of the inhibition if (but only if) the security right in question was created before the date of the inhibition.

Executors

There is no question but that a creditor of the defunct may inhibit the executor. He does this simply by raising an action against the executor in his capacity as such. Executry being a type of trust, the remarks made in relation to trusts above apply here also. Whether a decree against the defunct is a sufficient warrant for inhibition against the executor is uncertain. See further chapter 2.

Whether an inhibition against a defunct is effective against the executor is not certain. The problem is that at common law (ie prior to the Succession (Scotland) Act 1964) an executor did not administer the heritable estate, and so the question of the effect of inhibition as against him could not arise. The chief argument in favour of the view that the executor takes subject to the inhibition is that an executor is *eadem persona cum defuncto*. A full examination of this principle falls outwith the scope of this work, but it would not be controversial to say that the principle is one that is subject to many exceptions, and accordingly offers little guidance in the present matter. Under the old law, an inhibition did not take effect against the heir (see Stewart, p 554), and this may be taken as affording at least a weak presumption that an executor is likewise unaffected. A perhaps stronger consideration is that the executor's title is his confirmation, which as a judicial conveyance in his favour cannot be considered as a voluntary act of the inhibited party. In practice the issue does not often arise, for the executor will not usually seek to dispose of the heritage unless and until he has settled with the creditors of the defunct. See further chapter 3.

Heritable creditors

The subject of inhibition and heritable securities such as standard securities is considered in detail in chapter 9. In brief, an inhibition against the debtor is effective against a heritable creditor if it is dated before the creation of the security, but not otherwise. An inhibition against the heritable creditor by one of his creditors is good, because a heritable security is itself heritable property (save for certain rules of succession). It will thus bar the creditor from, for instance, assigning the security.

Receivers

Receivers are considered in chapter 11. In brief it is thought that a receiver is in essentially the same position as a heritable creditor, to the extent that the charge on which the receivership proceeds has attached to property affected by the inhibition.

Trustees in sequestration

Of all species of representative party, the trustee in sequestration is the only one whose position in relation to inhibitions is expressly regulated by statute. The 1985 Act, following the earlier legislation, provides that the title of the trustee is unaffected by any inhibition against the bankrupt, but that the inhibitor's preference against post-inhibition creditors is to be given effect to in the ranking. See further chapter 10.

Trustees under trust deed

The case of a voluntary trust for creditors poses special difficulties. The trust deed is a voluntary conveyance by the debtor and therefore is presumptively reducible by the inhibitor, in so far as it is a conveyance of the debtor's heritable estate. The matter is considered in more detail in chapter 10. The best view is that if the inhibitor has acceded to the trust, or if the trust has become 'protected' under the Bankruptcy (Scotland) Act 1985, then the inhibitor cannot challenge the title of the trustee, and matters proceed as in a sequestration, while if neither of these is the case the inhibitor can reduce. But on the strength of *Carlyle v Mathieson*[2] (1739) even a non-acceding inhibitor will lose his right of challenge if he takes no action until after the trustee has disposed of the estate.

Liquidators

Legislation concerning company law has always been approached by Parliament as a matter of English law, so it is not surprising that unlike the position for sequestration the Companies Acts are silent as to the effect of inhibition in a winding up. The matter is more fully discussed in chapter 11.

Administrators

Administration was introduced by the Insolvency Acts 1985 and 1986, and once again there is no provision for the effect of inhibition. The subject is considered in chapter 11 where the tentative conclusion is that the administrator is not free to dispose of the heritage without regard to the inhibition.

Judicial factors

A judicial factor may be appointed to administer heritable estate for a wide variety of reasons. On the basis of the argument that the factor's title to the estate does not derive from any voluntary act of the debtor it would seem that his title is unaffected by any inhibition against the

2 (1739) Mor 6971.

debtor and consequently that any disposal of the heritage made by him cannot be challenged on the ground of the inhibition. (See p 71.)

Foreign insolvency factors: (1) General

The case of foreign factors (using that term in a broad sense) poses special problems. Where the owner of heritable estate in Scotland is subject to the jurisdiction of a court furth of Scotland (eg a company incorporated in England or Germany, or an individual domiciled in those countries) the possibility arises of the court of domicile appointing some species of factor with power to administer immoveable estate wherever situate. The commonest case arising in practice is the English trustee in bankruptcy or liquidator or receiver. But sometimes a factor from an overseas jurisdiction makes his appearance.

In general Scots law (unlike the law of many other jurisdictions) will permit a foreign factor to realise immoveable estate in Scotland. (The leading case is *Araya v Coghill*[3] (1921).) But it is settled that in doing so the factor cannot always claim the privileges which are possessed by his Scottish equivalent. (See eg *Scottish Union and National Insurance Co v James*[4] (1886).) Thus the fact that a Scottish trustee in sequestration takes a title free of inhibition does not necessarily mean that his foreign equivalent will do the same. Furthermore it would seem—though here there is possibly room for argument—that the foreign factor cannot get round this rule by initiating a separate Scottish sequestration (etc) to deal with the Scottish assets. (The leading case here is *Goetze v Aders*[5] (1874).)

The only reported case which deals with this problem in connection with inhibition appears to be *Morley's Trustee v Aitken*[6] (1982). This involved an English bankruptcy. Lord Allanbridge, basing his decision on the English case of *Galbraith v Grimshaw*[7] (1910) and the Indian case of *Anantapadmanabhaswami v Official Receiver of Secunderabad*[8] (1933), held that the English trustee took the Scottish estate subject to the inhibition. The rule applied in those cases was that a foreign trustee in bankruptcy takes the estate only to the extent that it could have been 'assigned' by the bankrupt himself. ('Assign' is here used in a general sense.)

The difficulty here is that the law of inhibition provides that inhibition is a bar only to the voluntary acts of the debtor. Against other acts it is of no effect. A sale by a foreign factor will normally not be classifiable

---

3 1921 SC 462.
4 (1886) 13 R 928.
5 (1874) 2 R 150.
6 1982 SC 73.
7 [1910] AC 508.
8 [1933] AC 394.

as a voluntary act. The reason is that in general the factor is acting on the orders of a court of competent jurisdiction and so the sale by the factor will in general be involuntary as far as the debtor is concerned.

This difficulty in the decision of Lord Allanbridge can be better focussed if we consider the matter from a procedural point of view. Suppose that the factor does sell the heritable estate. If it is true that his right is subject to the inhibition, it will follow that the sale will be reducible at the instance of the inhibitor. But how could the inhibitor state a relevant case in the pleadings? The purchaser will plead that the sale was not the voluntary act of the debtor. The inhibition has not been contravened. As a consequence the inhibitor cannot instruct a relevant title to reduce. To such a defence it is difficult to see any reply.

Weighty though this objection is, the writer feels that the whole subject is of such complexity that he is unwilling to state any concluded view. A full discussion would consume more space than the writer is willing to devote to it. Very briefly, the sources of the complexity are threefold. In the first place, there is the complex nature of inhibition itself, so unlike other diligences. In the second place, those who evolved the rule in such cases as *Galbraith* certainly did not have in contemplation any diligence of the nature of inhibition. In the third place, the writer is respectfully of the opinion that Scots international private law in relation to foreign factors is undeveloped and unsatisfactory. But this is a matter which cannot be further analysed in a work of this nature.

One last point on *Morley's Trustee*. Lord Allanbridge founds of a dictum of Lord Dunedin in *Galbraith* to the effect that where there is already a 'process of universal distribution' in hand in England, English assets will not fall to the foreign factor. It is submitted that this is a rule of the conflict of laws which is separate from the rule mentioned earlier. Furthermore it is submitted that it is of no relevance to the question in issue. Lord Allanbridge held that an inhibition is a 'process of universal distribution' since it is 'only a first step prior to adjudication'. With respect, this is an error. It is doubtful whether even adjudication itself could be called a 'process of universal distribution'. It would not be 'universal' since it would not recover the moveable estate, nor even, very likely, all the heritage. Nor would it be a 'distribution' in any ordinary sense, since the creditors at large are not involved. A fortiori an inhibition cannot be so described. It is settled that inhibition is only a 'negative or prohibitory diligence'. (Erskine 2,11,13.) It is also misleading to call inhibition 'only a first step prior to adjudication' for that is to suggest that they are two steps of one diligence, related as arrestment is to furthcoming. On the contrary, inhibition and adjudication are two diligences, not two stages of one diligence.

As far as common law is concerned, therefore, the writer is unable to offer a general solution. Indeed the problem strikes him as one of the most difficult in the whole law of inhibition. It must be noted that ss 72,

185(4) and most of 426 of the 1986 Act, to be discussed below, do not apply to insolvency factors outwith the UK.

Foreign insolvency factors: (2) England and Northern Ireland

For more than a century there have been statutory provisions to give to the English insolvency factor a position, in relation to Scottish estate, superior to that which the common law would accord him. However, the courts have traditionally taken a very negative approach to these provisions, with the result that English factors in Scotland, and Scots factors in England, have been treated virtually as if they were from overseas. (See s 117 of the Bankruptcy Act 1883, s 117 of the Bankruptcy Act 1914, and the cases of *Galbraith*[9] and *Morley's Trustee*.[10]) To remedy this situation s 213 of the Insolvency Act 1985, now s 426 of the 1986 Act, was passed. Under subsection (1) there are general provisions, but subsection (2) provides that these do not apply to property rights, so they are probably irrelevant to inhibition. The meat of s 426 is in · subsection (4), which provides that statutory instruments may be made

> for securing that a trustee or assignee under the insolvency law of any part of the United Kingdom has, with such modifications as may be specified in the order, the same rights in relation to any property situated in another part of the United Kingdom as he would have in the corresponding circumstances if he were a trustee or assignee under the insolvency law of that other part.

Subsection (10) goes on to define 'insolvency law' as meaning

> in relation to Scotland, provision extending to Scotland and made by or under this Act, sections 6 to 10, 12, 15, 19(c) and 20 (with Schedule 1) of the Company Directors Disqualification Act 1986, Part XVIII of the Companies Act or the Bankruptcy (Scotland) Act 1985.

There are similar, and equally lucid, definitions in relation to England and Northern Ireland.

At the time of writing it seems that no order has yet been made under this section, but it seems likely that such an order will be made soon.

Section 426 is presumably meant to cover English and Northern Irish trustees in bankruptcy (plus the official receiver), liquidators, receivers and administrators. One serious difficulty, however, in interpreting the section is that it speaks of the 'trustee or assignee'. It is not apparent that

9 [1910] AC 508.
10 1982 SC 73.

liquidators, receivers or administrators are either 'trustees' or 'assignees'. But further comment would perhaps be premature until the relevant statutory instruments have been made.

There is also s 72 of the 1986 Act to consider. This derives from s 724 of the Companies Act 1985, which derived from s 7 of the Administration of Justices Act 1977, itself deriving from s 15(4) of the Companies (Floating Charges and Receivers) (Scotland) Act 1972. It states that

> a receiver appointed under the law of either part of Great Britain in respect of the whole or any part of the property or undertaking of a company and in consequence of the company having created a charge which, as created, was a floating charge, may exercise his powers in the other part of Great Britain so far as their exercise is not inconsistent with the law applicable there.

For general discussion of this provision see *Gordon Anderson (Plant) Ltd v Campsie Construction Ltd*[11] (1977) and an article by W. A. Wilson at [1977] JBL 160. It is odd that this provision has continued its existence independent of s 426. What its effect is in relation to inhibition is a matter of speculation. The *Gordon Anderson* case involved an arrestment, and it seems to have been held that the English receiver was in the same position in relation to the arrestment as a Scottish receiver would have been. Presumably the same is true, mutatis mutandis, in respect of inhibition. It should be noted that this provision (unlike s 426) cannot be invoked by Northern Irish receivers.

It remains to add that s 185(4) of the 1986 Act may be of relevance to the liquidation of English-registered companies. (But not Northern Ireland.) This subsection provides that the liquidation has the effect of a decree of adjudication in relation to immoveable estate in Scotland. It is doubtful, however, whether this provision is of much significance in relation to the law of inhibition.

Identification of parties

It sometimes happens that the designation of the party inhibited presents problems. For instance the name may be incomplete ('John Smith') instead of 'John Klaus Smith') or misspelt ('Mary Browne' instead of 'Marie Brown'). Similar problems may arise as to the address. Both name and address may change. Thus Marie Brown, on divorce, may revert to Marie Douglas, and may move house. A company may change its name and its registered office and place of business. Sometimes such problems cause no real difficulty as to identification, but very often they do. The writer understands that the Keeper is increasingly concerned with this problem. Two reasons in particular lie behind this concern. The first is the rapid increase in recent years in the use of inhibition. The second is the duty imposed upon the Keeper by the 1979 Act to enter on to title sheets 'adverse entries' in the Personal Register. The Keeper cannot carry out this duty where real problems of designation exist.

As a matter of practice, therefore, it is of the highest importance that law agents should ensure a full and correct designation. This is obviously in the interests of their own client as well as of other parties.

The writer is unable to offer much guidance as to what the law is in cases where a problem exists in the designation. Perhaps the problem can be divided into three. In the first place there may be an actual error in the designation. ('Mary' instead of 'Marie'.) The general approach of the courts in relation to diligence has been told that even minor errors of this sort are fatal, even if the error does not prevent the party being identified. Thus Bell (2,143) writes that 'all defects in the form of the diligence or in the mode of execution and publication are conclusively fatal'. See for instance *Walker v Hunter*[12] (1853). For a recent interesting example in the law of arrestment see *Richards and Wallington (Earthmoving) Ltd v Whatlings*[13] (1982). This is the familiar rule that diligence is strictissimi juris. But cases have occurred in relation to other diligences in which the courts have relaxed this rule. How strictly it would be applied in relation to inhibition is a matter of conjecture.

The second type of case is where there is no actual error but a serious incompleteness in the designation. Here again the law is a matter of conjecture. But there can be little doubt that where the incompleteness causes genuine ambiguity, the inhibition will be null. For a parallel case in the law of arrestment see *Lattimore v Singleton*[14] (1911).

The third type of case is where the designation is accurate and complete, but becomes inaccurate or incomplete by reason of change in circumstances, such as change of name or address. Here again the law is a matter of conjecture. Unlike the previous two types of case, no fault can be imputed to the inhibitor. On the other hand, it would be against all principle if loss should fall on a bona fide third party. Edinburgh readers may recall that in the late 1970s a property speculator against whom a large number of inhibitions were registered began to buy and sell under an alias. It is difficult to believe that those who purchased from him in good faith should have to suffer loss. There was no test case.

---

12 (1853) 16 D 226.
13 1982 SLT 66.
14 1911 2 SLT 360.

It may be that in this third type of case the criterion is that third parties are unaffected by the inhibition unless the identity was actually known to them or otherwise reasonably apparent. But as already stated, the law is unclear.

CHAPTER 6

Effect

Scope of chapter

This chapter considers the three effects of inhibitions. It is, however, not complete in itself, for certain particular issues will be examined in subsequent chapters, namely chapter 7 (ranking), chapter 8 (enforcement), chapter 9 (heritable securities), chapter 10 (bankruptcy) and chapter 11 (company law).

The effect of inhibition is to render voidable at the instance of the inhibitor all debts and deeds by the debtor, being both future (ie post-inhibition) and voluntary, which diminish, or may diminish, in favour of a third party, the value of the debtor's heritable estate. As Bell says (2.134),

> 'it is an injunction ... forbidding the debtor to grant any conveyance, or to execute any deed, or to incur any other debt, by which the creditor may be disappointed in obtaining payment or performance of the obligation whereupon the letters proceed, and prohibiting the public from giving the debtor credit, or receiving from him conveyances out of which such effect may arise.'

The effect of inhibition divides naturally into three. (a) Any conveyance of heritage is voidable. (b) Any security over the heritage is voidable. (c) Any debts which the debtor may contract are, in a question with the inhibitor, postponed to his claim in any process of ranking on the debtor's heritable estate. (The precise manner of this postponement requires further definition.) All these three effects are subject to the qualifications that the deed or debt be future and voluntary, and that the effects operate only in relation to affected estate.

Ranking rules in outline

Inhibition ranking can be fairly complex in practice, and so a separate chapter (chapter 7) has been devoted to it. But since inhibition ranking is an inseparable part of the effects of inhibition, it is appropriate to summarise it here. Inhibition ranking can be stated in two fundamental principles. (a) The inhibitor is to rank as if the post-inhibition deeds or debts (if any) had not taken place (ie he is to be neither prejudiced nor benefited by them. (b) Pre-inhibition creditors are to rank as if the inhibition did not exist (ie are to be neither prejudiced nor benefited by it).

Inhibition, adjudication, arrestment

It is sometimes supposed that inhibition is related to adjudication as arrestment is to furthcoming. Though there are similarities, the comparison is misleading. In the first place, arrestment and furthcoming are two stages of one diligence, whereas inhibition and adjudication are two distinct diligences. Thus it is perfectly competent to adjudge without first having inhibited, whereas it is not competent to raise a furthcoming without first having arrested. In the second place, arrestment, unlike inhibition is a seize diligence. A creditor who arrests thereby acquires a preference over the subject arrested. By contrast inhibition is only a freeze diligence, and the inhibitor acquires no preference, except as against post-inhibition parties, if any. What corresponds, in the field of heritable diligence, to arrestment is adjudication rather than inhibition. Adjudication, like arrestment but unlike inhibition, lays a nexus on the subject which confers a preference over it.

Future acts only affected

Inhibition strikes only at future acts, ie deeds and debts entered into after the date of the inhibition. Creditors whose claims were already in existence at the date of inhibition can be neither benefited nor prejudiced by it. Thus Stair (4,35,21): 'Inhibitions are only effectual against posterior voluntary rights.' Bankton (1,7,138): 'Inhibitions are only effectual against posterior voluntary debts and deeds.' Erskine and Bell are to the same effect. See also *Baird & Brown v Stirrat's Trustee*[1] (1872) and *Gordon v Campbell*[2] (1842). The rule, though a common law one, has also received statutory declaration. Section 155 of the 1868 Act declares that 'no inhibition shall have any effect against any act or deed done committed or executed prior to the registration' of the inhibition.

The reason that this rule is emphasised is that certain recent Sheriff Court and Outer House cases have been decided without this vital rule having been properly drawn to the attention of the court. These cases

1 (1872) 10 M 414.
2 (1842) 1 Bell's App 563.

were *George M Allan Ltd v Waugh's Trustee*[3] (1966), *Bank of Scotland v Lord Advocate*[4] (1977) and *Abbey National Building Society v Shaik Aziz*[5] (1981). In so far as these cases held that inhibition bestows a preference even against pre-inhibition creditors, they are in error, for the true rule is settled by earlier decisions, by unanimous institutional authority, and by statute. These three cases should therefore perhaps be regarded as being technically per incuriam. It should also be mentioned that these three cases are also contradicted in this respect by three other recent cases, namely *McGowan v Middlemas*[6] (1977), *Ferguson & Forster v Dalbeattie Finance*[7] (1981), and *Halifax Building Society v Smith*[8] (1985).

The test for whether a deed or debt is prior to an inhibition is the date of contract. In the case of a debt, the date when the debt is judicially constituted is thus not the relevant date. This rule has always been settled, and has recently been reaffirmed in *Halifax Building Society v Smith*[8] (1985).

Voluntary acts only affected

The rule is that among future acts only those which are voluntary are struck at. (See the quotations in the last paragraph.) This rule exempts from the effect of inhibition two classes of acts:

(a) Acts which the debtor is already under a legally enforceable obligation to perform. A typical example is where the debtor is inhibited after he has concluded missives to sell heritable property but before he has granted a disposition in implement of his obligation. The inhibition does not prevent the debtor from completing the transaction. Note, however, that it is the transaction which is exempted and not the property. Thus if the sale fell through, the debtor would not be able to sell to another buyer.

(b) Acts which are done by third parties. Thus an inhibition will not stop another creditor from adjudging (provided that the adjudication is led on a pre-inhibition debt). Similarly it will not prevent a sale by a heritable creditor under his power of sale, assuming again that the inhibition security was granted prior to the inhibition.

How far this second class can be extended is unclear. Thus the question arises in connection with sales by a curator bonis, a trustee in sequestration, a liquidator, a trustee under a voluntary trust deed, a

---

3 1966 SLT (Sh Ct) 17.
4 1977 SLT 24.
5 1981 SLT (Sh Ct) 29.
6 1977 SLT (Sh Ct) 41.
7 1981 SLT (Sh Ct) 53.
8 1985 SLT (Sh Ct) 25.

receiver, a judicial factor and an executor. Doubtless other examples could be thought of. Such cases create great difficulties. Some of them are discussed elsewhere: for trustees in sequestration and voluntary trustees under trust deeds, see chapter 10. For liquidators and receivers, see chapter 11. For executors, see chapter 5. It is thought that a curator bonis will be affected by an inhibition against the incapax. As for judicial factors, it does not seem to be possible to lay down a general rule, for judicial factors are of many different kinds. Each case must be considered individually. Thus it is thought that an inhibition against the absent party will affect a judicial factor loco absentis, whereas a judicial factor appointed under Sch 7 para 4, of the 1985 Acts would probably be able to sell free of inhibition. It may be relevant whether the factory has involved a sequestration (in the procedural sense of that term) but the matter is speculative.

Vests no real right

Inhibition is merely a 'negative or prohibitory diligence' (Erskine 2.11.13) which therefore 'vests no real right' (Bell 2.139). Though perhaps the identity is not obvious at first sight, this is really just another way of saying that inhibition strikes only at future voluntary acts, and that pre-inhibition creditors are to rank as if the inhibition did not exist. The proposition that inhibition vests no real right has two aspects, one 'substantive' and the other 'procedural'.

The first aspect is that inhibition can confer on the inhibitor no preference as against pre-inhibition creditors. Other diligences are very different in this respect. Thus poinding arrestment and adjudication all confer (subject to certain qualifications) a preference over the subject in question, as against all other ordinary creditors. This is because they all create some sort of real right. (What sort of real right is uncertain. In the case of arrestment there is even some authority that no real right is created. The point cannot be gone into here, but see Bankton 3.1.36, and an interesting article by Sim at 1984 SLT (News) 25.) Inhibition vests no real right and so gives no preference. The inhibitor merely has the right to disregard rights constituted after the date of the inhibition. He can do this because the recording of his inhibition is deemed to be known to all parties (see chapter 2) and so if they take deeds or debts from the debtor after that date they do so on known terms.

The second aspect of the fact that inhibition vests no real right is of a procedural nature. It is that an inhibition of itself does not entitle the inhibitor to participate in any process of realisation and distribution of the debtor's heritable estate (such as a sale by a heritable creditor). As Bell expresses it, 'the inhibitor has not . . . without adjudication or other diligence, any active title on which he can demand payment.' (2.139.) This follows from the essentially prohibitory nature of inhibition. In order to participate in such a process, the inhibitor must either use further diligence or be involved in a sequestration or liquidation. Why does this follow from the 'no real right' rule? Because by lacking a real right the inhibitor lacks a ranking. To say that he has no real right is to say that he has no right in the subject itself.

To summarise, the following propositions are virtually identical: (a) Inhibition creates no real right. (b) Inhibition cannot be enforced without either further diligence, or some form of bankruptcy process. (c) Inhibition strikes only at future voluntary acts. (d) Pre-inhibition creditors are to rank as if the inhibition did not exist. The importance of these propositions, and the fact of their identity, cannot be too strongly emphasised.

The first effect

The first effect of inhibition is to bar the debtor from disponing or otherwise conveying his heritable property. All transfers are barred, irrespective of their form (disposition, feu-disposition, assignation, etc.) and irrespective of whether the debtor receives a full price, or part price, or no price at all. Short leases granted by the debtor may, however, be exempted: see below.

Transfers which the debtor was already contractually bound to implement are not affected by inhibition. This is because such conveyances are not 'voluntary'. This has already been explained on page 70. Thus if A concludes missives on 1 May to sell land to B, with entry at 1 July, and on 1 June A is inhibited, the inhibition cannot prevent A from duly executing the disposition and delivering it on 1 July. The title B will get on duly recording or registering will be unimpugnable on the ground of the inhibition. (But while B may take the title in safety, he is entitled to reject it, on the ground that on the face of the registers, A was inhibited at the time of sale. The registers will date B's title from 1st July. B's title, therefore, while perfectly good, is not freely marketable. The question will be explored further in chapter 12.)

Dispositions or other deeds which violate the inhibition are not void, but are voidable at the instance of the inhibitor. This will be considered further in chapter 7.

Leases

Inhibition against a lessee was considered in chapter 4. Here we deal with inhibition against the lessor. The general rule is clear that inhibition prevents the granting of a lease. This may seem unfair on the unsuspecting lessee, but it must be recalled that the lessee has constructive knowledge of the inhibition (see chapter 2) and can easily discover the true position by a Personal Search. If he does not do so, he takes the lease at his own risk, just as happens if he omits to check the lessor's title is the Sasine or Land Register. (See *Trade Development Bank v Warriner & Mason*[9] (1980).)

The exception to this rule as stated in the authorities (Bell, 2.142, Stewart, p 562) is that inhibition does not strike at a lease for a 'fair rent' and for an 'ordinary duration'. (For an example of a lease not for a fair rent, see *Wedgwood v Catto*[10] 1817).) These were protean terms even in the nineteenth century, and changes since then in both the law and practice of leases has made them very nearly uninterpretable. The reason for the exemption was that a lease for fair rent and ordinary duration did not diminish the capital value of the lessor's heritable right. The inhibitor was therefore not prejudiced by the lease. This reasoning is perfectly sound and there is no doubt that it is still good law in the appropriate type of case. But the difficulties of modern application are as follows. (a) Inflation has meant that the lessor's interest is not protected without regular rent review. It is therefore suggested that in the modern context a 'fair rent' means not only a market rent as at the start of the lease, but also a reasonable provision for rent review—triennial, for instance. (b) When Bell was writing the standard duration of a domestic lease was twelve months, and that of an agricultural lease, nineteen years. Practice has changed, and the author feels unqualified to state what is 'ordinary' duration today for different sectors of the market. (c) Most problematic is the introduction of statutory protection of tenure. Dividing leases broadly into domestic, agricultural and commercial, the first two now generally attract security of tenure which has the effect of reducing the market value of the lessor's interest, often quite dramatically. Logically therefore a lease granted by an inhibited lessor in such circumstances should be reducible. But this leads to a paradox: Parliament, by conferring security of tenure, has made such leases reducible, whereas if no security of tenure had been conferred, the lease would have been irreducible. To this paradox the author can perceive no solution. One solution which is not available is to say that the security of tenure must be interpreted as being good against the inhibitor. The general rule for security of tenure conferred by statute is that it gives no protection where the title of the landlord is defective.

The second effect

The second effect of inhibition is to bar the debtor from granting any security over his heritable estate. Since the reform of the law of heritable security by the Conveyancing and Feudal Reform (Scotland) Act 1970 this has meant (subject to the next paragraph) that the debtor is disabled

9 1980 SC 74.
10 13 Nov 1817 Fac Coll.

from granting any standard security. The relation between inhibition and heritable security is discussed in chapter 9.

As a result of the.introduction from England of the floating charge, a new type of security over heritage has come into being. The effect of inhibition on floating charges is dealt with in chapter 11. The conclusion there arrived at is that an inhibition does strike at a subsequent grant of a floating charge, so far as the heritable estate of the debtor's company is concerned.

In the law of inhibition it is necessary to make a distinction between the debt and the security for the debt. (Such a distinction is indeed necessary in discussing securities from any angle.) Thus suppose that A owes money to B. C then inhibits A. A then grants a heritable security to B. Here the inhibition strikes at the security (second effect of inhibition) but not at the debt (third effect of inhibition) since the debt is pre-inhibition. Contrast this with the case where both the debt and the security are struck at by the inhibition. The two cases lead to different ranking: see chapter 7. (There is also the third case where the security is granted first, and the debtor is inhibited before he draws on the facility.)

The third effect

The third effect of inhibition is that debts contracted by the debtor after the date of the inhibition are postponed (in a certain defined manner) to the claim of the inhibitor in any process of realisation and distribution of the debtor's heritable estate. (In practice of course this means the distribution of the money proceeds of sale.) The leading case is *Baird & Brown v Stirrat's Trustee*[11] (1872). In this case it is of use to note carefully the terms of the final decree pronounced as well as the judgments. Although *Baird & Brown* can be described as the leading case, it should be observed that there is nothing in it which is not in earlier authority, and the Court expressly approves Bell's famous statement of the law. See also the early but important case of *Corsbie v Acheson*[12] (1631).

Before going into the third effect in more detail, it is as well to note two points. (a) Since inhibition is a diligence against heritage only, the third effect concerns only ranking on the heritage. Inhibition is no bar to post-inhibition debts in so far as the moveable estate is concerned. Thus if the estate is wholly moveable, the inhibition has no effect whatsoever. (b) The other point is how the ranking will actually occur, in which the

11 (1872) 10 M 414.
12 (1631) Mor 7017.

third effect is to be given effect to. Historically there have been many ranking processes. The commonest situation in the older cases was that all the creditors (inhibiting and non-inhibiting) would adjudge the heritage, and that the inhibition would be given effect to in the process of ranking-and-sale. This process (already for some time out of use) was abolished by the repeal of the Judicial Sales Acts by Statute Law Reform Act 1973. Nowadays the ranking process is usually a sequestration, a liquidation, or a sale by a heritable creditor. (Of these, only the first is necessarily judicial. Liquidation may be voluntary as well as compulsory, though recourse may always be made to the Court. The distribution of the proceeds of a sale by a standard security holder normally takes place extra-judicially, but in cases of difficulty will involve a multiplepoinding.)

The way that the third effect is to be applied is as defined in the Canons of Ranking (see chapter 7). In brief, the inhibitor is to rank as if the post-inhibition debt did not exist (ie he is to be neither benefited nor prejudiced by it), while the pre-inhibition creditors are to rank as if the inhibition did not exist (ie they are to be neither benefited nor prejudiced by it). This is done by dividing the ranking into two (imaginary) rounds. In the first round the parties are ranked as if the inhibition did not exist. In the second round the pre-inhibition creditors simply carry forward their first-round ranking unaltered. But the inhibitor draws back from the post-inhibition creditor sufficient funds to put him (the inhibitor) in the same position he would have been in had the post-inhibition debt not existed.

A simple example will illustrate the method. In a sequestration there is heritage worth £24,000. There are no moveables. There are just three creditors, A, B and C. A's debt is £24,000, B's is £12,000 and C's also is £12,000. B is the inhibitor. A's debt is pre-inhibition. C's debt is post-inhibition. Assume that the expenses have been accounted for. Then:

Round 1		Round 2	
A:	£12,000	A:	£12,000
B:	£ 6,000	B:	£ 8,000
C:	£ 6,000	C:	£ 4,000
	£24,000		£24,000

The above example (repeated in chapter 6 as example 1) is so straightforward as hardly to require comment. A, the pre-inhibition creditor, ranks as if the inhibition did not exist. B, the inhibitor, ranks as if C's claim did not exist. (If C's claim had not existed, A would have drawn £16,000 and B would have drawn £8,000.) It is important to observe that C is not wholly postponed to B, for C draws £4,000 even though B has not been paid in full. If B were to draw his full £12,000 at C's expense, B would *not* be ranking as if C's claim did not exist. Instead, he would be drawing *more* than he would have drawn if C's claim had not existed. Such a result would be absolutely contrary to the nature of inhibition, and all the authorities are clear against it. Lord Campbell was not exaggerating the strength and unanimity of the authorities when in *Gordon v Campbell*[13] (1842)—an important case—he said:

> 'The general rule, as laid down by all the institutional writers, ancient and modern, and founded on very solemn decisions, is, that inhibition being only a negative or prohibitory diligence, the inhibitor can neither be prejudiced nor benefited by a transaction *spreta inhibitione*.'

Relationship between the three effects

The three effects are really just one effect. What is barred is the alienation of the heritable estate. The first effect deals with actual alienation. The second deals with alienation of a slice of the value of the heritage by means of heritable security. The third deals with potential alienation, for the new creditor is entitled (if unpaid) to take a slice of the heritage for himself, whether by way of diligence or by way of bankruptcy process of some description.

The involuntary creditor

The third effect of inhibition bars the debtor from *contracting* debts capable of having a heritable ranking equal with that of the inhibitor. Some post-inhibition debts will, however, be found to be in some sense involuntary. Examples will be interest on pre-inhibition debts, additional parts of a pre-inhibition loan, and claims arising by the law of delict. Apart from such common law cases, there will be rates and taxes due to the local authority, the Inland Revenue, and the Customs and Excise. Although authority is sparse (for a good illustration, however, see *Scottish Waggon Co v Hamilton's Trustee*[14] (1906)) there is no doubt that such creditors, if genuinely involuntary, are exempt from the effect of inhibition.

---

13 (1827) 1 Bell's App 563.
14 (1906) 13 SLT 779.

Amount protected by inhibition

Inhibition operates in relation to (a) the principal sum, (b) interest thereon and (c) the expenses of the action. (See Stewart, p 554.) It does not operate in relation to other sums which may be due by the debtor to the inhibitor.

CHAPTER 7

Ranking

Scope of chapter

This chapter contains a discussion of inhibition ranking, with a number of worked examples. The chapter is not self-contained, for inhibition ranking is an indivisible part of the effects of inhibition (chapter 6) and the enforcement of inhibition (chapter 8).

The Canons of Ranking

The essence of inhibition ranking can be stated in two propositions: (a) the inhibitor is to rank as if the post-inhibition rights did not exist, ie he is to be neither prejudiced nor benefited by them; (b) pre-inhibition creditors are to rank as if the diligence did not exist, ie they are to be neither prejudiced nor benefited by it.

It may not at first sight be apparent how these rules are to be applied so as to produce a consistent result. The means of doing so were gradually developed in a series of Court of Session cases and finally codified by Bell in the Canons of Ranking. In practice both the courts and textwriters have treated these Canons as being of virtually statutory authority, and the present writer would respectfully adopt the same position. These Canons are reproduced here, except for the fifth, which is of lesser importance. They are to be found on p 413 of the seventh edition of the *Commentaries*.

> 1st CANON.—That the first operation in the ranking and division is, to set aside, for each of the creditors who hold real securities, the dividend to which his real right entitles him, without regard to the exclusive preferences.
>
> 2nd CANON.—That the rights of exclusion are then to be applied by way of drawback, from the dividends of those creditors whose real securities are affected by them; taking care that they do not encroach on the dividends of other creditors.
>
> 3rd CANON.—That the holder of such exclusive right is entitled thus to draw back the difference between what he draws upon the first

division, and what he would have drawn had the claim struck at by the inhibition not existed.

4th CANON.—That if the exclusive preference affects more than one real security, it is to be applied against those creditors only by whose ranking on their real right the holder of it suffers prejudice: against the last, for example, of the postponed creditors affected by it, in the first place; and so back, till the holder of the exclusion draws all that he would have been entitled to draw had the excluded claims not been ranked. If it affects a number of creditors entitled to rank pari passu, it will affect them proportionally to the amount of their several debts.

These Canons are so exactly framed that they require little comment. This chapter will be mainly concerned with giving illustrative examples.

Inhibition ranking is re-arrangement ranking

It is necessary to emphasise that there exists no system of inhibition ranking in the sense that there are systems for the ranking of, say, floating charges, or arrestments, or standard securities. Inhibition ranking is purely 'parasitic'. What it does is to re-arrange (by what is called 'draw-back') some existing ranking. Thus (Canon 1) the creditors are first ranked according to their infeftments or (in some cases) according to their arrestments. (See next paragraph.) The law of inhibition then makes certain adjustments to that ranking, so as to give the inhibition its effect. (And since inhibition strikes only at future debts and deeds, it will have no affect if there are no such debts or deeds.) Inhibition ranking thus necessarily presupposes at least two ranking rounds. Reflection will quickly show that there can never be any opposition between inhibition ranking and, say, arrestment ranking. Left to itself, inhibition prescribes no ranking whatsoever. It presupposes an existing ranking, arising out of the law of adjudication or arrestment or whatever. Put another way, there can be no Round 2 without a Round 1. This key feature of the law of inhibition is implied by, and implies, the fact that inhibition vests no real right. (See last chapter.) From this also follows the fact that if an inhibitor uses no further diligence (either actually, or constructively, through a sequestration or a liquidation) he cannot claim a ranking, for the law of inhibition cannot confer on him an adjusted Round 2 ranking if he is not present in Round 1, which can happen only if he has acquired a 'real security' or its equivalent. (See next paragraph.)

Canon 1 refers to 'real securities'. Bell was thinking of heritable securities or adjudications. In his day the question of inhibition ranking almost always arose in connection with a Judicial Ranking and Sale, a process long unknown in practice and finally abolished by the repeal of the Judicial Sales Acts by the Statue Law Reform Act 1973. If taken literally, the requirement that in order to enter the first round the creditors must have 'real securities' would deprive the inhibitor of his preference (if any) in sequestrations, in liquidations, and (after arrestment) in distributions by heritable creditors after compulsory sales. But this would be a misinterpretation. In sequestration and liquidation, all the ordinary unsecured creditors are thought of as acquiring (through the trustee or liquidator) an equal right to the assets. (See eg *Baird & Brown v Stirrat's Trustee*[1] (1872), and chapters 10 and 11.) As for distributions (either directly, or through a multiplepoinding) by a heritable creditor, the inhibitor gets his 'real security' by arresting the fund. Whether, strictly speaking, arrestment creates a real right is a matter of debate, with authorities on both sides of the question. The point is not relevant for present purposes, since arrestment by attaching the fund and establishing a ranking is sufficient to set up Round 1. Indeed, in recent cases the question has not so much been whether arrestment in such cases is sufficient as whether it is necessary at all, ie whether the inhibitor could be admitted to Round 2 without being present in Round 1. (It must be stressed that he cannot. See further next chapter.)

Example 1

This is the example given towards the end of the last chapter. There is a sequestration, with three creditors, A, B and C. A claims £24,000 and B and C claim £12,000 each. There are no moveables. The heritage (after deduction of the expenses) realises £24,000. B is the inhibitor. A is pre-inhibition. C is post-inhibition. In Round 1 the parties are ranked pari passu as if the inhibition did not exist. What the pre-inhibition creditor (A) draws in this round he will take through to Round 2, unchanged, for he must rank as if the inhibition did not exist. But in Round 2 the inhibitor (B) must *draw back* from the post-inhibition creditor (C) the amount necessary to put him (B) in the position he would have been in if C's claim had not existed. Now, if C's claim had not existed, B would have drawn £8,000. Why? Because in that case the £24,000 fund would have been divided pari passu between just A and B, with A drawing £16,000 and B drawing the balance. So:

	Round 1		Round 2
A:	£12,000	A:	£12,000
B:	£ 6,000	B:	£ 8,000
C:	£ 6,000	C:	£ 4,000
	£24,000		£24,000

1 (1872) 10 M 414.
2 (1842) 1 Bell's App 563.

Note in this example that the post-inhibition on creditor (C) still draws a large sum even though the inhibitor has not been paid in full. The inhibitor is entitled to rank as if the post-inhibition debts and deeds did not exist, but to more than this he is not entitled. See *Gordon v Campbell*[2] (1842).

Is inhibition a 'security' for ranking purposes?

The last example was devised so as not to involve any non-inhibited estate. But in practice in liquidation and sequestration there is always a large amount of non-inhibited estate. All the moveable estate will fall into this category, and often part of the heritable estate will also fall into it. The existence of such non-inhibited estate creates a ranking difficulty. If the inhibitor has by his inhibition a preference over all or part of the heritable estate, is he bound, for ranking purposes, to make a deduction in calculating the amount of his claim against the remainder of the estate? This depends on whether an inhibition is to be classified as a 'security' for the purposes of the relevant legislation (currently Sch 1(5) of the Bankruptcy (Scotland) Act 1985, applied to liquidation by para 4.16 of the Insolvency (Scotland) Rules 1986). It is important, in approaching this question, to bear in mind that the meaning of the word 'security' in this context has been accorded a wider sense by the courts than the word has in its ordinary usage. Thus while it may be said that an inhibition is not a right in security in the ordinary sense, this does not necessarily imply that it is not a 'security' for the purposes of the statutes regulating liquidation and sequestration.

Judicial authority on this question does exist, but unfortunately it is conflicting. In *Hay v Durham*[3] (1850) and *Mitchell v Motherwell*[4] (1888) it was held that inhibition is to be regarded as a 'security' for this purpose. On the other hand in the case of *Scottish Waggon Co v Hamilton's Trustee*[5] (1906) it was held that it is not a 'security'. On ordinary principles the former authorities should be preferred on the ground that they are more numerous and proceed from higher courts. As against this it can be said that the issue does not seem to have been seriously argued in those cases, while it was so argued in the latter case. In addition it is necessary to observe that the latter case, though only a decision of the Outer House, has established itself as one of the leading cases on the law of inhibition. A great deal could be said on this matter. For instance in *Scottish Waggon*

3 (1850) 12 D 676.
4 (1888) 16 R 122.
5 (1906) 13 SLT 779.

Co there was not a full citation of earlier authority. Furthermore in *Halifax Building Society v Smith*[6] (1985) the earlier cases were approved. On the other hand this was only by way of obiter dictum, and it was not noticed that *Scottish Waggon Co* is to a contrary effect.

In view of these difficulties it is with only some hesitation that the writer expresses his opinion that the decision in *Scottish Waggon Co* is to be preferred. What, it seems to the writer, tips the balance in favour of that case is that to require an inhibition to be ranked as a 'security' would contravene the settled rule that the benefit of an inhibition is personal to the inhibiting party and is not to enure to the benefit of other creditors. If the inhibitor is to be required, in ranking against the non-inhibited estate, to deduct from the amount of his claim the amount of draw-back he received in ranking on the inhibited estate, the real effect would be that at least part of the benefit of the inhibition would enure to the benefit of other creditors.

It remains to be said that if this approach is taken, there is an incidental advantage in that it simplifies the calculations necessary by the liquidator or trustees in drawing up the Scheme of Division.

The following examples are calculated on the basis that the decision in *Scottish Waggon Co* is correct.

Example 2

The situation is as in example 1, with this difference only that there is £12,000 of non-inhibited estate.

	Inhibited estate (*As example 1*)	Non-inhibited estate	Total
A:	£12,000	£6,000	£18,000
B:	£ 8,000	£3,000	£11,000
C:	£ 4,000	£3,000	£ 7,000
	£24,000	£12,000	£36,000

In certain cases the application of this rule may apparently lead to a situation in which the inhibitor draws more than 100 p in the £. This is a circumstance which is always liable to arise when Sch 1(5) of the Bankruptcy (Scotland) Act 1985 (or its forerunners) is inoperative, and it need hardly be said that no creditor can receive more than 100 p in the £. In such a case the excess should be returned to the post-inhibition parties, rather than distributed equally among the creditors. The following example illustrates the point.

Example 3

In a sequestration there are three creditors, A, B and C, claiming £18,000, £9,000 and £9,000 respectively. B is the inhibitor. A is pre-inhibition and C is post-inhibition. The inhibited estate is £24,000 and the non-inhibited estate is £6,000. Leave the expenses out of account.

	Inhibited estate		Non-inhibited	Total
	Round 1	Round 2	estate	
A:	£12,000	£12,000	£3,000	£15,000
B:	£ 6,000	£ 8,000	£1,500	£ 9,500
C:	£ 6,000	£ 4,000	£1,500	£ 5,500
	£24,000	£24,000	£6,000	£30,000

What has happened here is that B has drawn £500 more than his claim. This £500 must therefore be returned to the other creditors. But to whom, exactly? Clearly, the whole £500 must go to C, the post-inhibition creditor. This is so not only on equitable grounds, but as a direct result of the law of inhibition. This prescribes that pre-inhibition parties (here, A) are to rank as if the inhibition did not exist. If any part of the £500 excess went to A, this rule would be violated, for A would be drawing more than he would have drawn if there had been no inhibition. So the whole £500 goes to C, producing a final division of £15,000 to A, £9,000 to B and £6,000 to C.

Sequestration: calculation of Round 1

In the above examples, all the creditors enter Round 1 with a pari passu ranking. This is because sequestration operates as some sort of notional attachment on behalf of all creditors. (For the effect of sequestration in doing this, see *Baird & Brown v Stirrat's Trustee*[7] (1872) per Lord President Inglis.) Two variants on this are possible. The first is where there is a sequestration or liquidation in which one of the creditors for some reason enters Round 1 with some sort of unequal ranking (eg he

7 (1872) 10 M 414.

holds a standard security). The second variant is where the ranking process is one which, unlike sequestration and liquidation, does not automatically confer on all creditors a notional attachment. The typical case here is the distribution of the free proceeds after a sale by a heritable creditor, which may occur extra-judicially, or by means of a multiplepoinding. Each variant will be looked at in turn.

Example 4

There is a sequestration with three creditors, A, B and C, each claiming £12,000. B is the inhibitor. A is pre-inhibition. C is post-inhibition, and took a standard security in exchange for his loan to the debtor. The inhibited estate is worth £18,000. Disregard expenses.

	Round 1	Round 2
A:	£ 3,000	£ 3,000
B:	£ 3,000	£ 9,000
C:	£12,000	£ 6,000
	£18,000	£18,000

This ranking derives directly from the Canons of Ranking. In the first round we apply to its full extent C's real right. B then draws back from C enough to put him in the position he would have been in if C's claim had not been in existence. A's position in the ranking should be carefully noted. He is to rank as if the inhibition did not exist. Consequently C's standard security is to have full effect as against him. The standard security is fully effective as against all parties except the inhibitor. Note also that the inhibitor is not to benefit from the standard security. Hence it is that B draws £9,000 but no more.

Example 5

This example is a variation on the last example. Let all the facts be the same, except that C's claim is pre-inhibition. What is post-inhibition is the grant of the standard security. In other words, the debtor borrowed the money from C before the inhibition, and later (and without a pre-inhibition obligation to do so) granted a security for the loan. In such a case it is very likely that the standard security will be reducible by the trustee in sequestration as a fraudulent preference, but assume for the sake of argument that this is not so. Then:

	Round 1	Round 2
A:	£ 3,000	£ 3,000
B:	£ 3,000	£ 6,000
C:	£12,000	£ 9,000
	£18,000	£18,000

The explanation is that the inhibition strikes at C's security but not at his debt. So in calculating the draw-back the hypothesis is the non-existence of the standard security, but not the non-existence of the debt. On this hypothesis B would have drawn £6,000 (as would A and C also). Once again, C's standard security is fully effective as against A.

Multiplepoinding

The other type of case referred to above where not all the creditors necessarily enter Round 1 with an equal ranking is where the distribution process is one which (unlike sequestration) does not automatically confer on all creditors some sort of notional equal attachment. The main judicial process which has this characteristic is the multiplepoinding. As is well known, multiplepoinding does not operate as a diligence for all creditors. It merely gives effect to such lawful rights in the fund in medio as have already been regularly constituted. The main extra-judicial process which also has this characteristic is the distribution of the free proceeds after a sale by a heritable creditor. These two cases often in practice coincide, for in cases of complexity a heritable creditor will wish to secure judicial exoneration by raising a multiplepoinding. (For further discussion, see the following chapters.)

The practical effect of these theoretical considerations is that outwith the context of sequestration and liquidation no creditor has a right to participate in a distribution process unless he has some right in the fund, by security, by assignation or by diligence. Thus a creditor who holds a standard security, or who has an adjudication, or who has arrested the fund after it has assumed liquid form, has an effective attachment and a defined ranking and can thus participate. Other creditors cannot. For these purposes an inhibition is not sufficient diligence. 'The inhibitor has not . . . without adjudication or other diligence any active title on which he can demand payment.' (Bell, 2.139.) An inhibition entitles the user to rank as if the post-inhibition debts and deeds were not in the field. It does nothing more. Inhibition ranking is only a re-arrangement ranking, and, as the Canons of Ranking make clear, no creditor can enter Round 2 who has not been in Round 1, and no one can be in Round 1 without a real right or its equivalent.

Example 6

There is a sale by a heritable creditor, A, and a multiplepoinding of the proceeds, which, after expenses, amount to £24,000. A's debt is £12,000, and B, C and D are all separately creditors to a like extent. C is the inhibitor. A and B are pre-inhibition. D is post-inhibition. D arrests. B and C do not, nor did they adjudge before the sale. In the multiplepoinding B and C will draw nothing. A will draw £12,000, and D will draw the same.

Example 7

As example 6, but B also arrests, simultaneously with D. C still draws nothing. A draws £12,000, while B and D draw £6,000 each. Note that the inhibition has no effect as between B and D. It will be recalled that the rule is that pre-inhibition parties are to rank as if the inhibition did not exist.

Example 8

As in example 6, but B, C and D all arrest, simultaneously.

	Round 1	*Round 2*
A:	£12,000	£12,000
B:	£ 4,000	£ 4,000
C:	£ 4,000	£ 6,000
D:	£ 4,000	£ 2,000
	£24,000	£24,000

In this example, all the arrestments rank pari passu is Round 1 because they were used simultaneously. The same result would emerge if they were used at different times but equalised by the operation of Sch 7, para 24 of the 1985 Act. In the next examples we will suppose the arrestments not to be simultaneous, and also that for one reason or another Sch 7, para 24 of the 1985 Act does not come into play.

Example 9

As in example 6, but B, C and D arrest, in that order.

	Round 1	*Round 2*
A:	£12,000	£12,000
B:	£12,000	£12,000
C:	—	—
D:	—	—
	£24,000	£24,000

Here the inhibition is of no benefit to C, for he would still have drawn nothing if D had not been in the field.

Example 10

As example 6, except that D, B and C arrest in that order.

	Round 1	*Round 2*
A:	£12,000	£12,000
B:	£ —	£ —
C:	£ —	£ —
D:	£12,000	£12,000
	£24,000	£24,000

Once again the inhibition proves worthless. This result at first sight seems odd, because the inhibitor draws nothing while the post-inhibition creditor draws his full claim. But it is as prescribed by the Canons of Ranking, and indeed is a particularly instructive example, showing the true nature of inhibition. (See Bankton 1, 7, 147 for a comparable example.)

Example 11

A property is sold by a heritable creditor (A) and realises (after deduction of expenses) £36,000. There is a multiplepoinding of the proceeds. The other creditors are B, C and D, and all four creditors claim £12,000. C is the inhibitor. A is pre-inhibition. Both B and D are post-inhibition. B adjudged the property before the sale. D and C arrest the fund, in that order.

	Round 1	*Round 2*
A:	£12,000	£12,000
B:	£12,000	£12,000
C:	£ —	£12,000
D:	£12,000	£ —
	£36,000	£36,000

This example illustrates the Fourth Canon. Where there are several post-inhibition parties, the draw-back is not equally against all. The contribution is levied from them according to their ranking. Accordingly, since B was, by his adjudication, preferred to D, who merely arrested after sale, the draw-back operates against D. Only if D's first-round share had been insufficient to meet the draw-back would B have been affected, as in the next example.

Example 12

As example 11, except that C's claim is £18,000. This produces a final ranking of £12,000 to A, £6,000 to B, £18,000 to C and nil to D.

Example 13

In a sequestration the heritage realises £30,000. Ignore the moveables. There are five creditors. A, B and D claim £12,000. C and E claim £6,000. C is the inhibitor. D and E are post-inhibition. A holds a standard security.

	Round 1	*Round 2*
A:	£12,000	£12,000
B:	£ 6,000	£ 6,000
C:	£ 3,000	£ 6,000
D:	£ 6,000	£ 4,000
E:	£ 3,000	£ 2,000
	£30,000	£30,000

This example again illustrates the Fourth Canon. D and E are pari passu and therefore must contribute rateably to the drawback. Note that rateable contribution means that D's absolute contribution is twice E's.

Multiple inhibitors

In the foregoing examples there has been only one inhibitor. In practice, however, it is often the case that there is more then one inhibitor. The existence of more than one inhibitor can create difficult problems. Rather surprisingly there appears to be almost no authority as to how multiple inhibitors are to be ranked. The correctness of the solutions given in the following paragraphs cannot therefore be guaranteed, but the writer puts them forward as being in harmony both with the general principles of the law of inhibition and with the spirit of Scots ranking law as a whole.

Example 14

The first type of case is very simple. Both inhibitions strike at the same claim. Thus suppose that in a sequestration there are three creditors, A, B and C. A and B have both inhibited, and both inhibitions strike B's claim. A's debt is £40,000. B and C both claim £20,000. The heritage is sold for £30,000.

	Round 1	Round 2
A:	£15,000	£20,000
B:	£ 7,500	£10,000
C:	£ 7,500	nil
	£30,000	£30,000

This is a simple case. C's first round draft is at the second round transferred rateably to A and B, with the result that the two inhibitors receive all that they would have drawn had the post-inhibition claim not existed. Note in particular that it makes no difference whether we apply A's draw-back first, and B's second, or the other way round. The result in either case is the same. The source of the difficulties adverted to above is that this happy outcome is not obtainable in all types of cases, as the next example will show.

Example 15

In this example, the first inhibition (A) strikes at two claims (C and D), whilst the second inhibition (B) strikes only at the later of these (D). The order of events would thus be as follows. First, the claims of A and B would have been in existence. Thereafter, A inhibited. Later, C's claim arose. Then B inhibited. Finally, D's claim came into being. The result, of course, is that A's inhibition strikes at both C and D whilst B's inhibition strikes only at D.

Let A, B and D each claim £6,000. C's claim is £12,000. The fund available to these creditors is the balance remaining after a sale by a standard security holder, and it amounts to £18,000. The four creditors all arrest this fund (which of course is necessary, for otherwise they could not enter the ranking at all). The order of arrestments is C, D, B, A. This yields the following first round:

	Round 1
A:	nil
B:	nil
C:	£12,000
D:	£ 6,000
	£18,000

At this first round, C ranked primo loco because he was the first to arrest. D ranked next, being the next arrester. These two arrestments exhausted the fund, leaving nothing for A or B. The problem now arises as to how to apply the rights of drawback of A and B. A different result emerges according to whether we apply A's drawback before B's, or the other way round. If we apply A's first, we get the following result, 'Round 2' showing A's drawback and 'Round 3' showing B's drawback.

	Round 2	Round 3
A:	£ 6,000	£ 6,000
B:	nil	nil
C:	£12,000	£12,000
D:	nil	nil
	£18,000	£18,000

The explanation of this result is that the fourth Canon of Ranking directs that A's drawback must be exercised in the first instance against the less preferred of the two struck-at claims. In this case this means that A draws back in the first instance from D (since D arrested later than C). This has the effect of reducing D's draft to zero. Accordingly, when we come to apply B's drawback in Round 3, there is nothing left.

A very different result emerges if we apply the rights of drawback the other way round, so that B's drawback is applied first. Thus:

	Round 2	Round 3
A:	nil	£ 6,000
B:	£ 6,000	£ 6,000
C:	£12,000	£ 6,000
D:	nil	nil
	£18,000	£18,000

Which method is therefore to be applied? One response would be to say that since A is the first inhibitor, his drawback should be applied first. Superficially attractive though this is, it conflicts with the settled rule that inhibitions 'are not preferable according to their dates'. (Stewart, p 561.) Or as Bell puts it (2, 141): 'Inhibitions do not give preference according to the rule *prior tempore potior jure*.' A second approach to the problem would be to say that B should draw back first, on the basis that this is in essence a case of 'catholic' and 'secondary' creditors. The settled system of catholic and secondary claims is that the preference of the more preferred creditor is to be exercised in such a manner as will be least prejudicial to the secondary claimant. In this instance this would mean that A's inhibition is to be applied so as to cause least loss to B.

The objection to this second approach is that it penalises C, making him suffer as a result of an inhibition (B's) to which he is not subject. Accordingly the writer proposes that the correct solution is neither of these. It is submitted that it is necessary to avoid applying either draw-back before the other. The correct solution, it is submitted, is that A and B should in the first instance draw back rateably from the claim to which they are both preferred (D). (This is simply applying the method of example 14 above.) Once that is done A can draw back from C for any shortfall there may still be. Thus:

	Round 2	Round 3
A:	£ 3,000	£ 6,000
B:	£ 3,000	£ 3,000
C:	£12,000	£ 9,000
D:	nil	nil
	£18,000	£18,000

What has happened here is that in Round 2 the two inhibitors have drawn back rateably from D. This gives A and B £3,000. B can claim no further draw-back. A still has a draw-back from C, and this is given effect to in Round 3.

CHAPTER 8

Enforcement

Enforcement where no breach

If an inhibition has been contravened by no debt or deed, then there is nothing to be enforced. In that case the inhibition is, as regards further procedure and ranking, a nullity. This fact derives from the nature of inhibition as being a purely prohibitory diligence. Unlike other diligences, such as poinding or arrestment or adjudication, it does not give to the creditor any form of real right over the debtor's property. It merely gives the creditor a certain form of preference over other parties acquiring rights after the date of the inhibition. If no such parties exist, no preference can exist. 'Inhibition, in a question with them [pre-inhibition parties] has simply no effect at all.' (Lord Mackenzie in *Scottish Waggon Co v Hamilton's Trustee*[1] (1906).)

From one perspective, this may seem paradoxical. If the inhibition is successful, it stops the debtor from granting certain rights. But in that case, it is without effect. Conversely, it only has effect when it is unsuccessful, ie where rights are granted in breach. So it might seem that when an inhibition is effective, it is without effect, and it only has effect when it is ineffective. This paradox is more apparent than real. Although inhibition is spoken of as 'prohibiting' certain things, this expression is a little misleading. It does not prohibit in the sense that an interdict prohibits. The debtor in fact remains free to grant rights, and other parties to receive such rights, but only conditionally, so that the granting of such rights cannot prejudice the inhibitor. Thus in a sense it matters nothing to the inhibitor whether his inhibition is 'obeyed' or not, for in truth there is nothing to be 'obeyed'. Thus the granting of post-inhibition debts and deeds does not mean that the inhibition has been unsuccessful, for such debts and deeds do not affect the inhibitor. Conversely, if no such debts and deeds are in fact granted, this does not mean that the inhibition has been 'successful'. Inhibition (unlike interdict) can never be either successful or unsuccessful. It simply has

---

1 (1906) 13 SLT 779.

the effect that all debts and deeds granted after its date have attached to them inescapable conditions. It is up to the parties involved whether they wish to be subject to such conditions or not.

When, therefore, there is no breach of inhibition, the inhibition has no effect and confers no preference. To enforce his claim the inhibitor is thus in exactly the same position as other creditors and must proceed by further diligence or by initiating or participating in the sequestration or liquidation of the debtor.

Recovery where there is breach

The remainder of the chapter deals with the enforcement of an inhibition where there has been contravention. By way of generalisation it can be said that inhibition being purely negative and prohibitory, the fact of contravention, while it vests in the inhibitor certain rights, does not of itself give him the means of enforcing those rights. Those rights must be enforced by one or more of the following processes:

(i)   reduction;
(ii) adjudication;
(iii) arrestment;
(iv) sequestration or liquidation.

Which process, or which combination of processes, the inhibitor should adopt depends on the circumstances of the case.

Reduction

In general a contravention of an inhibition is reducible at the instance of the inhibitor. (i) As regards the first effect of inhibition, the inhibitor may reduce the relevant deed of transfer. Typically this will be a disposition, but it may also be a feu disposition, a feu contract or an assignation, or, occasionally, a discharge or a renunciation. Where the transaction stands only on the footing of missives, there can be little doubt that the reduction may be directed at the missives. (ii) As regards the second effect of inhibition, the inhibitor may reduce the deed which creates the security. Since the 1970 Act the standard security has been the only form of security over heritage. The only significant exception to this rule is the floating charge. Whether a floating charge over heritage granted by an inhibited company can be reduced will be considered in chapter 10, but the writer's opinion is that it can be. (iii) As regards the third effect of inhibition, the question of reduction does not normally arise. It is only if the post-inhibition creditor obtains an adjudication on the basis of his post-inhibition debt that the inhibitor needs to reduce. In such a case the reduction is directed against the adjudication. (Stair, 4,35,21; Erskine, 2,11,11.)

Procedure

The general procedure involved in reduction will not be discussed here, since it belongs to civil procedure as a whole. Only the distinguishing features will be mentioned. The first of these is that the conclusion of the summons should expressly state that the reduction is sought ex capite inhibitionis. These words must also be incorporated in the extract decree. The reason for this is explained below, but, in brief, it is to show that the reduction is in its effect not 'catholic' but only ad hunc effectum. Next, the extract decree must be recorded in the Sasine Register or registered in the Land Register, according to whether the subjects in question are on the one register or the other. See the 1924 Act, s 46, applied to the Land Register by s 29(2) of the 1979 Act. Occasionally (see chapter 9) a discharge of a standard security can be reduced on the ground that the party granting the discharge was inhibited, and in this (uncommon) case the reduction can be recorded or registered only if within five years of the discharge. (See s 41(2) of the 1970 Act.)

If the title is in the Land Register, the action of reduction should conclude for both (1) reduction and (2) rectification. See an article by the writer at 1986 SLT (News) 125 on the subject of the reduction of heritable titles.

Effect of reduction

Reduction ex capite inhibitionis operates ad hunc effectum, ie does not operate as a catholic reduction. That is to say, the deed or conveyance reduced does not become null as against all parties, but only as against the inhibitor. As against other parties it is of full force and effect. Thus suppose that A inhibits B and B thereafter dispones to C, and A reduces the disposition. This does not render C's title null. Ownership does not pass back from C to B. C is still owner, vest and seised as of fee. The effect of the reduction is simply that A is entitled to proceed as if ownership were still in B, and that this entitlement prevails over the claims of C, of C's creditors, and of those taking from C by voluntary deed. The reduction thus operates as a declarator that the contravention, while not absolutely void, can be treated as void by the inhibitor. Thus Ross (*Lectures*, p 488 of vol 1 of edition of 1822): 'When lawyers say that a debt or deed is reduced *ex capite inhibitionis*, it is not meant that the deed is really void, for, *quoad* every other person but the inhibitor it remains perfectly sufficient, because reductions *ex capite inhibitionis* are, properly speaking, declarators.' Thus Erskine (2,11,14): 'Even where the deed is actually avoided ex capite inhibitionis, the reduction has no effect, but in favour of the inhibitor himself.'

Entry in the Land Register

The entry of the decree of reduction in the Land Register will reflect this fact. Since the reduction does not annul the grantee's infeftment, his name should not be removed from the Title Sheet. He remains as the registered proprietor. The Keeper must of course give effect to the decree in the Title Sheet. The Land Registration (Scotland) Rules do not give any guidance as to how this should be done. The writer's suggestion is that the most convenient place to note the decree is in the Charges Section of the Title Sheet. The Keeper will be aware that the reduction is not a catholic one because the extract will expressly state that it is ex capite inhibitionis.

The function of reduction

As has been stated, reduction does not have any property consequences, in the sense that the reduction does not actually annul any infeftment or title of property. It is simply declaratory that the inhibitor is entitled to proceed as if the offending deed had not been granted. Thus A inhibits B and B thereafter dispones to C. A reduces the disposition. This enables A to proceed as if B were still the owner. In other words, A can now adjudge the property. Without the reduction he could not have done this, for the property belongs not to B but to C, and the general rule of diligence is that diligence can be used only against the property of the debtor. Thus the reduction enables A to use diligence against C's property. This may seem hard on C but of course he took the subjects with knowledge of the inhibition.

When necessary

'To give inhibition effect, a process of reduction must actually be brought upon it ... There is no exception to this rule but in the competition and ranking of creditors, where, to save time and expense, the Lords are accustomed to give effect to this diligence by way of execution.' (Ross, Lectures, 1822 edn, 1,477.) This is still good law today. Naturally, reduction is very often in practice unnecessary, because an extrajudicial settlement is arrived at. But this does not affect the doctrine.

The main problem is as to what counts as a process of ranking of creditors. The main example in Ross's day was the process of judicial ranking and sale, whereby heritable property was brought to a judicial sale, and the proceeds distributed to the creditors according to their lawful ranking. This process has long since disappeared, and was finally abolished by the Statute Law Reform Act 1973. The modern ranking processes, in which reduction can be dispensed with, are sequestration, compulsory liquidation, and multiplepoinding. The last of these tends to arise when a heritable creditor has sold under his power of sale, and wishes judicial authority as to how the proceeds should be distributed. Receivership does not seem to have the attribute of a judicial ranking process, for it is not normally a judicial process at all and in addition most creditors are excluded from it. The new process of company administration may be such a process, being both judicial and in the interests of creditors generally. But it is such a strange process that judgment must be suspended. A voluntary trust deed for creditors, so long as it remains unprotected, is not such a process. If and when it becomes protected, it would seem to become a ranking process of the appropriate kind. It is true that it is extrajudicial, but matters proceed as in a sequestration. Perhaps the most problematic process is voluntary liquidation. See chapter 11.

Reduction on its own

Reduction on its own is of limited value. The inhibitor's debt is still unpaid. Reduction may in practice bring about extrajudicial settlement, but failing that the inhibitor must follow up his reduction by further diligence, or by participating in a process of distribution, such as a sequestration. It should be noted, however, that one benefit bestowed by a bare reduction is interruption of prescription of the inhibition.

Where inhibition is on dependence only

In practice the question of reduction arises when the inhibition is in execution, or, though used on the dependence, it has been converted into an inhibition in execution by decree in favour of the inhibitor. But in theory the question must be asked as to whether a party who holds only an inhibition on the dependence can, at that stage, reduce a deed contravening the inhibition. Erskine writes (2,11,3):

> An inhibition upon a depending action can have no effect towards annulling deeds granted by the debtor after that diligence, till the dependence be closed by a decree in favour of the pursuer; because, until such decree be recovered, it is uncertain whether the inhibitor be truly creditor to the party inhibited.

This must be correct, but it may be wondered whether it might not be convenient to let a reduction be raised and then at once sisted until the principal action is completed.

Adjudication

Adjudication is the only means whereby a creditor can obtain by diligence a real right in the heritable estate of his debtor. It is therefore the natural next step for an inhibitor to take, and Bell rightly describes (at 2.135) adjudication and inhibition as being 'co-operative diligences, the latter acting as a prohibition for guarding those subjects over which a real right may be constituted by adjudication'. The great benefit of inhibition is that it operates as a blanket diligence, which can be used without the need for the sometimes laborious process of discovering what heritable estate the debtor holds. This process has to be gone through before an action of adjudication can be raised, since adjudication must specify the subjects to be adjudged. But though inhibition is a rapid process, and has a blanket effect, its defect is that it gives no real right, and thus does not give the inhibitor any active title to extract payment from the estate. For this adjudication is necessary.

As a general rule it can be said that an inhibitor must always adjudge, in the event that his inhibition does not succeed in inducing the debtor to make voluntary settlement. There are only two exceptions to this general rule. The first is where the heritage is sold by a third party and thus converted into a moveable fund. In this case the need for further diligence is not removed, but the further diligence required is not adjudication but arrestment, in view of the now moveable nature of the asset. This will be dealt with more fully later. The other exception is where the debtor is sequestrated or in liquidation. As is well known, after the commencement of sequestration and liquidation further diligence by individual creditors ceases to be possible. The trustee or liquidator is deemed to adjudge on behalf of all creditors.

Though in general an inhibition must be followed up by adjudication, the two processes are not two steps of one diligence (like arrestment and furthcoming) but rather two independent diligences. Hence it is that a creditor is free to adjudge without first having inhibited.

Adjudication will be treated of in a separate chapter (chapter 13).

Arrestment

Inhibition must be followed up by arrestment where the heritable subjects have been converted into a moveable fund as a result of a sale. The sale here in question is of course not a sale by the debtor, for that would be reducible, and the subjects still open to adjudication. The sale in question is a sale which is not prevented by the inhibition and which therefore puts the subjects beyond the reach of adjudication. The typical example is a sale by a heritable creditor, such as a standard security holder. Such a sale will be unchallengeable by the inhibitor, at least if the security was constituted before the date of the inhibition, as is normally the case.

If before the sale the inhibitor has adjudged, the arrestment will be unnecessary, for he will be paid according to his ranking as the holder of a judicial heritable security. Arrestment is necessary only where there has been no adjudication.

The arrestment will of course only be effectual if there is a free surplus arising after both expenses have been met and the claims of secured creditors have been satisfied.

Chapter 9 will deal further with sale by a heritable creditor where there exists an inhibition against the debtor. The situation can also arise in other ways, however, for instance where there is a sale by a judicial factor.

Sequestration and liquidation

Where the debtor is in sequestration or liquidation further procedure by the inhibitor is generally speaking neither necessary nor competent. The trustee or liquidator is deemed to have used diligence on behalf of all creditors according to their respective rights. This subject will be further considered in chapters 10 and 11.

Need for further procedure

The fact that an inhibition of itself does not give the inhibitor a direct right to payment from the debtor's estate is a fact of great importance. It derives from the fact that inhibition is merely a negative or prohibitory diligence and vests in the inhibitor no real right in the debtor's estate. As Bell puts it, 'the inhibitor has not . . . without adjudication or other diligence any active title on which he can demand payment.' (Commentaries, 2,139.) There has been a certain tendency in some of the modern cases to confuse inhibition with adjudication in this connection. Adjudication gives to the adjudger a real right, a judicial heritable security over the subjects in question. Inhibition is quite different in its effect, and much of the confusion which has ensued from some of the modern cases could have been avoided if the learned judges had been informed as to the differences between inhibition and adjudication.

The cases which (it is respectfully submitted) confuse inhibition with adjudication and thus treat inhibition as if it gave to the inhibitor a real right without further procedure are almost all cases dealing with the distribution of the proceeds of sale by a heritable creditor, and will be mentioned therefore in chapter 9. For present purposes the most important are *Armour and Mycroft Petitioners*[2] (1983) and *Halifax Building Society v Smith*[3] (1985). The first of these dealt with the distribution of the proceeds of sale by a receiver. The second was the more usual case of a sale by a heritable creditor, but its importance lies in the fact that the judgment of the learned Sheriff Principal gives the question serious attention, though the conclusions at which he arrived were (it is submitted) not entirely correct.

The characteristic situation is where there is a sale by a heritable creditor after the debtor has been inhibited, and the question arises as to how the free proceeds are to be distributed. The law of inhibition prescribes two notional rounds of ranking. At the first round the various creditors, including the inhibitor, are ranked according to the securities and diligence which they hold, entirely ignoring the inhibition. At the second round the inhibition draws back from the post-inhibition creditors, if any, in the manner described in chapter 7. It follows that if the inhibitor has no security or diligence other than the inhibition itself then he will receive nothing, just as other lawful creditors of the debtor will receive nothing from the free proceeds, unless they hold a security or diligence.

In a sense this rule is no more than the great principle of law that where one party (here the selling security holder) holds money for a second party (here the debtor and former owner of the subjects) then the first party is not obliged to pay that money to the second party's creditor's, unless those creditor's have right to it either by diligence or by the voluntary act of the second party himself. (See *Henderson v Begg*[4] (1889) for a well-known example of an application of this principle.) This principle, of fundamental importance in the general law of debt, means that an inhibitor must have adjudged before the sale or arrested after it in order to have a claim on the free proceeds.

An alternative way of viewing the matter is to commence with the Canons of Ranking. The notional second round takes the inhibitor's first round ranking and augments it by contributions exacted from the first round rankings of the post-inhibition creditors, if any. The first round ranking, both of inhibiting and non-inhibiting creditors, are, of course, ascertained without reference to the effect of inhibition. Consequently a creditor who holds nothing but an inhibition cannot enter the second round because the second round is merely an adjustment of the first round, and in the first round such a creditor cannot participate at all,

---

2 (1983) SLT 453.
3 1985 SLT (Sh Ct) 25.
4 (1889) 16 R 341.

because at the first round the ranking is done without reference to the inhibition.

Yet another way to view the matter is to consider that an axiom of the law of inhibition shall not prejudice parties whose claims were already in existence at the date of the inhibition. This rule would be violated if the inhibitor were to be allowed, by virtue of his inhibition and nothing else, to rank.

These rules apply regardless of the procedural context. For instance the proceeds of sale by a heritable creditor may be distributed either with or without a multiplepoinding. But the mode of distribution will be the same in either case. Just as an inhibitor who holds nothing but an inhibition could not demand payment direct from the heritable creditor out of the free proceeds, so he could not demand it from the fund in medio in a multiplepoinding. In either case he has no title to payment except by adjudication or arrestment. 'A claim in a multiplepoinding has in itself no effect. The multiplepoinding does not supersede the necessity for diligence.' (Green's Encyclopaedia, vol 10, para 283.) 'A claim in a multiplepoinding has by itself no effect as diligence.' (*Walker's Civil Remedies*, p 1240.) The only difference which requires comment between a multiplepoinding and an extra-judicial distribution is the fact that in the case of arrestments the multiplepoinding has the effect of making furthcoming unnecessary.

Halifax Building Society v Smith[5] (1985) was a noteworthy case, displaying considerable learning from the bench, and correctly formulating the rules as to draw-back by an inhibitor against post-inhibition parties. The case, however, fell into the error of supposing that an inhibitor is in titulo to compear and rank without further diligence. It is hoped that the foregoing remarks, brief though they are, will sufficiently explain the correct rule. Something more about this interesting case will, however, be said in chapter 9.

Armour and Mycroft[6] was a less typical case. A company was inhibited and afterwards went into receivership. The receivers sought permission from the Court to sell the company's heritable estate free from the inhibition, in terms of s 21 of the 1972 Act (now s 61 of the 1986 Act). The Court granted this permission, and directed that any proceeds of sale that might be surplus to the claims of the chargeholders fell to be paid directly to the inhibitors. This case involved some special difficulties, since it raised the question of the meaning of the statutory provision that the attachment of a floating charge is subject to the 'effectually executed diligence' of other creditors 'on the property' of the debtor

5 1985 SLT (Sh Ct) 25.
6 1983 SLT 453.

company. (See ss 1(2) (a), 15(2) (a) and 20(1) (b) of the 1972 Act, now 463(1), of the Companies Act 1985 and ss 55(3) and 60(1) (b) of the 1986 Act.) The meaning of this provision in relation to inhibitions will be further considered in chapter 11. For the present it is sufficient to say that on the facts of the case it is clear that the inhibition did not affect the floating charge, and that the rights of the chargeholders were clearly preferable to those of the inhibitors. The Court was thus quite correct in authorising the receivers to sell free of the inhibition and to apply the proceeds of sale in the first instance to the claims of the chargeholders (subject, of course, to any preferential claims). The error (it is respectfully submitted) of the Court lay in its direction as to payment of any surplus direct to the inhibitors. The inhibitors had no title to such surplus, for essentially the same reasons as apply in the case of a sale by a heritable creditor. The proper course for the inhibitors in this case was to adjudge before the sale or to arrest after it.

Exceptions

The rule that, in order to establish a title to payment, the inhibitor must use further diligence, is subject to certain exceptions. The first exception is where the sale is by certain types of representative parties, such as a trustee in sequestration. The second exception, whose standing is less certain, is where there has been a sale by the debtor in contravention of the inhibition.

Exception 1

The first exception arises typically in insolvency law, where a trustee or liquidators or similar is appointed. But it can arise in certain other cases, such as where the debtor has died and there is an executor appointed and confirmed. These cases are considered in chapter 5. In some of these cases the representative party is free to sell the heritable notwithstanding the inhibition, while in other cases he is not so free. Where he is not so free, the exception does not apply. But where he is free to sell, the inhibition is in some sense defeated. If the inhibitor can adjudge before the sale or arrest after it, he should do so, and failure to do so will, it is thought, mean that he has missed the boat, so that the inhibition is without affect. (Cf a sale by a heritable creditor.) But in some cases such diligence is not competent. Typical examples are sequestration and liquidation. In such cases it is thought that the exception of necessity applies, namely that the inhibition will take effect in the ranking notwithstanding the absence of further diligence. In the case of sequestration this is expressly provided by statute, but it is thought that it applies also in other cases such as liquidation. The rule can be summed up by saying that where further diligence is not competent it is not necessary either.

Precisely what cases fall under this exception is a matter of some difficulty. Sequestration does so. Liquidation is less clear. Trust deeds for creditors also qualify provided that either the inhibitor has acceded or the trust has become a 'protected' trust under the Act of 1985. Executry is less clear. Diligence against an executor is generally incompetent for six months after the death, and this fact would suggest that executry falls under the exception, ie that the executor must give effect to the inhibition in the distribution to creditors notwithstanding the want of further diligence. But the matter is not free from difficulty. Other cases are also obscure.

Exception 2

The second of the two exceptions emerges from three old cases, *Monro of Pointzfield*[7] (1777), *Lennox v Robertson*[8] (1790), and *McLure v Baird*[9] (1807). The rule, or alleged rule, seems to be that when an inhibitor sells heritage contrary to inhibition, the price is deemed to be payable to the inhibitor directly, or rather, to speak more precisely, such part of the price as will meet the inhibitor's claim. A full discussion of these cases would take up more space than they perhaps deserve. (For analysis, see an article by the writer at (1982) 27 JLSS 13 and 68.) What stands in the way of accepting the rule is that in none of these cases was the alleged rule actually put into effect. In *Monro* the purchaser himself had acquired right to the inhibition, so that for ranking purposes the purchaser and the inhibitor were the same party. In *Lennox* the inhibitor had arrested the price in the hands of the purchaser. In *McLure* the inhibitor had adjudged. If the rule is to be accepted, therefore, it is not so much by virtue of these authorities as by virtue of Bell's acceptance of the rule (Comm 2,139). But the rule seems contrary to principle, and so in the absence of any clear case in which an inhibitor has been held, without further procedure, to be entitled to direct payment by the purchaser, the alleged rule must be regarded as being of doubtful status. The only safe course for the inhibitor to take is to reduce and adjudge, as indeed the inhibitor did in *McLure*. This latter case is indeed an excellent illustration of the manner in which inhibition operates. Another creditor, who had not inhibited, attempted to adjudge the subjects as well as

7 (1777) Mor Inhib App No 3.
8 19 Nov 1790, Hume 243.
9 19 Nov 1807 Fac Coll.

the inhibitor. It was held, in conformity with the settled rules of inhibition, that the adjudication by the non-inhibiting creditor was of no effect, since the transfer of the property was valid as against all parties but the inhibitor.

Heritable securities

Scope of chapter

This chapter deals with the law of inhibition in its relation with the law of heritable security. It thus covers two types of case. The first, and most common case, is where the debtor in the security is inhibited, whether before or after the granting of the security. The second type of case, much less common, is where the inhibition is against the creditor in the security.

Pre-inhibition security

In the most common case the debtor is inhibited after he has granted the heritable security. In that case the inhibition has no effect against the security (except possibly in regard to future lending, for which see below). This follows from the general rule that inhibition affects only the future voluntary debts and deeds of the debtor. As a result the security holder is free to exercise his remedies, both statutory and common law, unprejudiced by the inhibition. The usual remedy adopted is sale. Thus a sale by a heritable creditor is unaffected by any inhibition which is later in date than the original granting of the security. (This is so at common law, and is confirmed by s 26(1) of the 1970 Act, which states that a sale by a standard security holder discharges the subjects of all securities and diligences not preferable to the standard security itself.) This doctrine has two facets. In the first place the heritable creditor's *power* of sale is unaffected. In the second place the heritable creditor's *ranking* as against the proceeds of sale is unaffected.

So much, then, for the position of the heritable creditor. We now must consider what the position is of the inhibitor when the heritable creditor exercises his power of sale. This subject is one of some complexity, and its exposition presupposes the general analysis of the ranking effects of inhibition which the writer has attempted to furnish in chapters 6 and 7. The law can be summarised in the following propositions. (1) The inhibitor has, by virtue of his inhibition alone, no right to claim any part of the proceeds of sale, and accordingly will receive nothing unless he takes further steps of procedure. This is so irrespective of whether the proceeds are distributed judicially (by multiplepoinding) or extrajudicially. Thus in the case of multiplepoinding the creditor who holds nothing but his inhibition can qualify no title to compear. (2) To establish a right to be paid from the proceeds of sale the inhibitor must either have adjudged before the sale or have arrested after it. (3) This having been done, the inhibitor is paid according to the Canons of Ranking, as described in chapter 7. This is effected by two imaginary ranking rounds. In the first round the inhibition is disregarded, and the compearing creditors are ranked according to their infeftments, the creditors who have no real security being ranked on the balance according to their arrestments. In the second round the inhibitor draws back from the post-inhibition creditors such sum as is needed to put him into the position which he would have been in had the post-inhibition creditors not ranked. If there are no post-inhibition creditors (as is very often the case) the inhibition is, naturally, of no effect.

Though the propositions in the foregoing paragraph represent (it is submitted) an accurate summary of the law, the position is complicated by the fact that certain recent sheriff courts cases, and one Outer House case, are not entirely consistent with these propositions, and are, moreover, inconsistent with one another. The cases are *George M. Allan v Waugh's Trustee*[1] (1964), *Bank of Scotland v Lord Advocate*[2] (1977), *McGowan v Middlemas*[3] (1977), *Abbey National v Shaik Aziz*[4] (1981), *Ferguson & Forster v Dalbeattie Finance Co*[5] (1981) and *Halifax Building Society v Smith*[6] (1985). The second of these was an Outer House case, the others all in the Sheriff Court. There has been no decision of the Inner House in this area.

All these cases were similar in their facts. First there was a heritable security. Later another creditor inhibited the debtor. There was a sale by the heritable creditor. The question was then how the creditors should be ranked on the proceeds of sale. In all the cases the form of process was a multiplepoinding, except in the first of the cases, where there was a sequestration. In the first of the cases the security was by way of ex facie absolute disposition. In the second it was by way of bond and disposition in security. In the others it was by way of standard security.

These cases are discussed in some detail by the writer in an article at

1 1966 SLT (Sh Ct) 17.
2 1977 SLT 24.
3 1977 SLT (Sh Ct) 41.
4 1981 SLT (Sh Ct) 29.
5 1981 SLT (Sh Ct) 53.
6 1985 SLT (Sh Ct) 25.

(1982) 27 JLSS 13 and 68, except for the last of them, which the writer analysed at 1985 SLT (News) 125. The following remarks summarise the arguments in those articles.

In the first place the inhibitor must qualify a title to be paid other than the fact only of his inhibition, since 'the inhibitor has not ... without adjudication or other diligence any active title on which he can demand payment.' (Bell 2,139.) This means that the inhibitor must either have adjudged before the sale or arrested after it. Alternatively if the debtor has been sequestrated or liquidated the inhibitor will by that very fact acquire a direct title to be paid. In all this the inhibitor is in exactly the same position as any other creditor. It should be said that Stewart (p 559, note 1) is to a contrary effect. But he cites Bell, 2, 139, so it is clear that he had misread Bell on this point.

When a creditor wishes payment from the free proceeds of sale, what he is seeking is payment by his debtor's debtor, for after sale the heritable creditor becomes debtor to the ex-owner to the extent of the surplus. Now it is a fundamental feature of our law of debt that a creditor cannot require payment from his debtor's debtor except where he can instruct a title by (1) assignation or (2) security or (3) diligence. Accordingly the mere fact that X is owed money by the former owner of the property gives to X no right to be paid by the former heritable creditor out of the proceeds of sale. To have such a right he must show a good security, or show that the surplus has been assigned to him, or use diligence. Such is common law, and the current statutory provision dealing with the distribution of the proceeds of sale, namely s 27 of the 1970 Act, is in conformity with the common law in this respect.

One or two details apart, it makes no difference if the fund is distributed judicially by multiplepoinding rather than extrajudicially. The process of multiplepoinding is not designed to alter the general principles of ranking, but on the contrary it is designed to give effect to them. The only special effect of multiplepoinding that requires notice is that where the fund has been arrested the decree in the multiplepoinding supersedes (or rather has the effect of) furthcoming.

Accordingly the creditor who has inhibited but not adjudged must arrest the proceeds of sale in the hands of the heritable creditor. This need for arrestment is not really a surprising one. Even if there is no sale, so that the heritable estate remains in forma specifica, inhibition on its own does not constitute an attachment in the strict sense of that term. After using inhibition, the creditor is only half way home, and if he does nothing further, the debtor's estate may still be carried off by the more timeous diligence of other creditors. (*Vigilantibus non dormientibus jura subveniunt.*) As Lord President Campbell put it in *Lennox v Robertson*[7]

---

7 19 Nov 1790, Hume 243.

(1790), inhibition 'is only a prohibitory diligence, and the inhibitor to make out his preference must adjudge'. Or as Stewart puts it (p 566): 'As inhibition is only a prohibitory diligence, not a real security, the inhibitor can only have the benefit of it by adjudication.' These remarks are accurate so long as the estate is unsold. Read literally, they would imply that after sale, if the inhibitor has not already adjudged, he can do nothing, for he is too late. But of course the inhibitor may, like any other creditor, arrest, and this will supply the place of adjudication, though it may not give him quite the same ranking.

As already stated, it makes no difference if the heritable creditor raises a multiplepoinding. (In which case of course the heritable creditor is both real and nominal raiser. It is naturally also possible, but less common, for another party qualifying an interest to be the real raiser in the name of the heritable creditor.) The parties who are, without further procedure, in titulo to compear in the process are the real raiser, the nominal raiser (if different), the creditors holding real security, and the ex-owner. This being so, what steps must the other creditors of the ex-owner take in order to compear? If the ex-owner does not himself lodge a claim (and this is commonly the case) then his creditors simply arrest the free proceeds (before the multiplepoinding is raised) or the fund in medio (thereafter). (It must be remembered that a depending multiplepoinding does not operate as a sist of diligence quoad those who are not, or not yet, parties to it.)

The nexus created by such arrestment (being an attachment) has the effect of entitling such arresting creditors to become parties to the multiplepoinding in their own right, and to lodge claims. It is then open to them to plead any preferences to which they may have right (which, in the case of the inhibitor, will mean the claim to exclude post-inhibition creditors). But it is not, as has already been mentioned, competent for the ordinary unsecured creditors of the ex-owner simply to lodge claims without arrestment. As the author of the article in *Green's Encyclopaedia* concisely puts it, 'a claim in a multiplepoinding has in itself no effect. The multiplepoinding does not supersede the necessity for diligence.' (3rd edn, vol 10, para 283.)

There is indeed an exception to this rule. Where there is a party who is entitled to claim in a multiplepoinding (eg the ex-owner, or even the heritable creditor himself) and that party has actually lodged a claim ('the primary claimant'), a creditor of such primary claimant can himself lodge a claim without arrestment, provided that his debt against the primary claimant is constituted or at least based on a liquid document of debt. Such a claim is technically known as a 'riding claim'. It is sometimes stated (eg *Maxwell's Practice of the Court of Session*, p 374, *Mclaren's Court of Session Practice*, p 674) that a creditor of a claimant in a multiplepoinding can himself claim *only* by way of a riding claim. This is a mistake. The error doubtless arose from the learned authors copying the headnote of the report in *Gill's Trustees v Patrick*[8] (1889), which is to that effect. Indeed, the headnote goes even further and states that a creditor of a party who is *entitled* to claim (whether or not he has in fact claimed) can himself claim only by way of riding claim, a doctrine which is doubly mistaken. In truth the headnote entirely misrepresents what was decided in the case. Indeed, it is hardly even necessary to go so far as analysing the judgments in order to perceive that the alleged rule is quite contrary to principle. The very nature and origin of multiplepoinding illustrate the point. The process of multiplepoinding was instituted, as is well known, for no other purpose than to give relief to double distress, by ranking the arrestments made in the hands of the fundholder by the creditors of the party primarily entitled to the fund. It would thus be entirely contrary to the whole purpose of the process if arrestment were excluded after the compearance of the primary claimant. Indeed such a rule would lead to the bizarre situation where many creditors would be excluded from the fund altogether, if, not having constituted their debts or holding liquid documents of debt, they did not qualify to lodge riding claims. (Whereas, under the law as it truly is, such creditors are free to arrest on the dependence of actions of constitution.) The reader who wishes to pursue this matter further is referred to *Gill's Trustees* (above) and to *Royal Bank v Stevenson*[9] (1849).

The inhibitor must therefore adjudge before the sale or arrest after it, except where the ex-owner is subject to sequestration or liquidation. In that case the inhibitor acquires, by the force of the process, a direct right to payment, according to his ranking. This was the situation in *George M Allan*[10] (above). In the other cases cited towards the beginning of the chapter the process was multiplepoinding and in them it would appear (though the reports are not as full as they might be) that the inhibitor had neither adjudged nor arrested. Consequently he had no title to compear. None of these cases, however, dealt with this point, except for *Halifax Building Society v Smith*.[11] In this case the learned Sheriff Principal did consider the point and came to the conclusion that the inhibitor fell to be paid from the proceeds without either adjudication or arrestment.

In general the judgment in this case is of a high quality and repays study. But on the particular point under consideration it is wrongly decided. This is so for the reasons already given, but two further points require to be made. The first is that the Canons of Ranking preclude an

---

8   (1889) 16 R 403.
9   (1849) 12 D 250.
10   1966 SLT (Sh Ct) 17.
11   1985 SLT (Sh Ct) 25.

inhibitor, without adjudication or arrestment, from ranking in a multiplepoinding. The learned Sheriff Principal makes the perhaps natural assumption that if the inhibitor arrests then the ranking must be governed either by the law of ranking of inhibitions or by the law of ranking of arrestments. These he takes as different systems of ranking. The conclusion is then inevitable that to require arrestment by the inhibitor would be to mix oil and water. After all, so it would appear, if the inhibitor must arrest, what is the point of the inhibition, and what role could be given to the rules of inhibition ranking? This line of thought, plausible though it may appear, is based on an incomplete apprehension of the Canons of Ranking. As was stated in chapter 7, inhibition ranking is purely a system of the *rearrangement* of an existing ranking. Thus so far is it from being the case that inhibition ranking and arrestment ranking might be mutually exclusive, the former actually *presupposes* the existence of the latter, or of some other ranking by way of attachment. This is the whole tenor of Canons 1,2 and 3. Inhibition can never be given effect to in Round 1 of the ranking. By its very nature, and as expressly provided for by the Canons, it operates solely by way of draw-back in the second round. The first round is determined by the ordinary rules of attachment-ranking, according to the general law of heritable security, adjudication and arrestment. It is only by having a first round ranking that the inhibitor can enter the second round.

The other point arising out of the *Halifax* case concerns the suggestion in that case that an inhibition is a 'security' in terms of s 27 of the Act of 1970, which is the current statutory provision dealing with the distribution of the proceeds of a sale by a heritable creditor. The learned Sheriff Principal points out that the word 'security' in that section is not qualified by the word 'heritable'. Accordingly it is capable of including inhibition. Even if this were a correct interpretation of s 27 it would lead to the curious consequence that that section had unintentionally altered the law of inhibition. But with respect it is a mistake. The draftsman rightly omitted the word 'heritable' since he did not wish to exclude various miscellaneous rights such as arrears of feuduty, groundannual, statutory charges under the Housing (Scotland) Acts, and similar statutory provisions, attached floating charges, adjudications and so forth.

Furthermore the suggestion that in s 27 'security' could include inhibition would lead to an impossible result. For if inhibition is a security then a fortiori so is an arrestment. This would mean that s 27 directed the fundholder to pay to arresting creditors without furthcoming, a consequence which is obviously absurd.

Moreover, and pursuing the same line of reasoning, if inhibition were a 'security' within the meaning of s 27 then it would follow that the inhibitor would be entitled to direct payment from the fundholder in preference to all other unsecured creditors, including anterior creditors. This result would be directly contrary to the Canons of Ranking, and, in this context, is contrary to the remainder of the learned Sheriff Principal's judgment, in which he holds that the inhibitor is to have no preference as against anterior creditors.

The writer apologises for the length of the discussion above, which he feels is made necessary by the importance of the matter. No disrespect is intended to the learned Sheriff Principal in the *Halifax* case, whose judgment, apart from this single point, is admirable.

We must turn now to the question of how the inhibitor is to rank on the free proceeds. Here there are two misconceptions into which it is possible to fall. One is that the inhibitor has in relation to the surplus no right which is preferable to the right of any other unsecured creditor. The other misconception is that his right is preferable to that of all other unsecured creditors. The truth lies between these two extremes. The right of the inhibitor is no better, merely by virtue of his inhibition, than the right of other creditors whose claims were anterior to the inhibition, while on the other hand the inhibitor is entitled to exclude those creditors claiming on the strength of debts contracted after the date of the inhibition. Of the cases cited towards the beginning of this chapter only *Halifax* states this rule accurately. The others are either unclear or fall into one or other of these two misconceptions. The weight of such cases is much diminished by the fact that they were, in the first place, by and large decided per incuriam, and in the second place, they contradict each other as much as they contradict the correct doctrine. No disrespect is intended to the learned judges concerned, who found themselves confronted with a subject of considerable technical complexity, and were afforded a less than full citation of and analysis of authority. They may take comfort in the fact that in the leading case of *Baird and Brown v Stirrat's Trustee*[12] (1872) so eminent a judge as Lord Deas found himself unable to grasp the rules of inhibition which Lord Kinloch, in the same case, described as 'so firmly established and so trite' that he could not understand how they were not followed at an earlier stage in the litigation.

The correct procedure is therefore for the inhibitor to be ranked according to his adjudication (if he has one) or his arrestment. No adjustment of this ranking is necessary or even competent unless also ranked are parties who are classifiable as posterior creditors. Where such creditors are ranked, there is a second round in which the inhibitor draws back from such creditors such sum as is necessary to put him in the

12 (1872) 10 M 414.

position he would have been in had they not ranked. The details are as laid down in the Canons of Ranking, and the reader is further referred to chapter 7.

Post-inhibition security

We turn now to the less common case where the heritable security has been granted after the inhibition. In that case the security is itself a violation of the inhibition (second effect of inhibition). In such a case the correct course for the inhibitor to take is to reduce the security, and to adjudge. Alternatively he may adjudge first and then reduce (an order of proceeding not available in the case of breach of inhibition by disposition). The difficult question is what the position of the inhibitor is if he fails so to act and then finds that the security holder is selling the property by virtue of his power of sale. Though not common, this is a situation which does come up, and there is little guidance from the authorities. The answer is probably that the subjects continue to be affected by the inhibition notwithstanding the sale, so that the inhibitor could still reduce and adjudge even when the property was in the hands of the purchasers. The latter would not be protected under s 41 of the 1924 Act (as applied by s 32 of the 1970 Act) since they could not claim to be in good faith, having either actual or constructive knowledge of the inhibition (cf s 18 of the Court of Session Act 1868). In practice the agent for the purchaser will, or should, refuse to settle so long as the pre-security inhibition appears in the Search.

Security for future advances

It sometimes happens that while the heritable security was granted before the inhibition, part of the lending which is secured was made after the inhibition. For instance A borrows £10,000 from B and grants to him a standard security for all sums due and to become due. Then A is inhibited by C. Thereafter A borrows a further £5,000 from B. What is the effect of the inhibition in relation to this further £5,000?

This is a matter of considerable practical importance, but there exists no clear authority. Though the difficulty is not a new one, in earlier times it did not often arise. A few words of historical explanation are necessary here. Prior to 1970 the general rule was that a heritable security could not secure advances made subsequent to its creation. Thus if this rule had been strictly adhered to the problem with which we are dealing could not have arisen. But the rule was found inconvenient and was circumvented in two ways. One was the bond of cash credit and disposition in security, which was introduced by statute (33 Geo III c 74, s 12, later s 7 of the Debts Securities (Scotland) Act 1856). The other was a disposition ex facie absolute but truly in security, which was functionally a heritable security but formally a transfer of the dominium utile. The statutory provisions relative to the bond of cash credit expressly stated that all advances made under such a security were to be deemed, by a statutory fiction, to have been made as at the date of its creation. This meant that the difficulty with which we are now concerned could not arise, for the effect of the statutory fiction was that post-inhibition advances were to be considered as if they were pre-inhibition advances. This inevitable conclusion was duly drawn in *Campbell's Trustees v De Lisle's Executors*[13] (1870). But in the case of the ex facie absolute disposition there was, of course, no such statutory provision. Nor is there any reported case, and the only authority appears to be that of Stewart. At p 565 Stewart writes: 'It is thought that the disponee [ie the creditor] is not entitled after intimation of the inhibition to him to make further advances. Such advances are really debts contracted after the inhibition.'

This passage is of particular interest today not because of ex facie absolutes, which are now almost entirely things of the past, but because standard securities are really in this respect in the same boat. They too are normally securities for all sums due and to become due, but unlike the bond of cash credit there exists no statutory provision whereby future advances are protected from the effect of supervening inhibition.

Stewart's view that post-inhibition advances are adversely affected by the inhibition seems correct. What is functionally the position is that the creditor is making a new loan upon further security, and there seems no reason why he should be protected from the effects of the inhibition any more than any other creditor who takes such security. (It is true that Burns expresses a different opinion (p 483) but on a point of this nature the authority of Stewart is high. In addition Burns does not argue the matter.)

Stewart qualifies his position by saying that the inhibition affects the creditor only after it has been intimated to him. It is difficult to see any ground for this qualification. Inhibition takes effect against other parties without intimation, and there seems to be no reason for exemption in this case. Moreover it is submitted that such an exemption is precluded by statute. Section 18 of the Court of Session Act 1868 provides that at the moment of recording the inhibition 'shall be held to be duly intimated and published to all concerned'. This seems conclusive.

It might seem that if this is the law, it is unfair to the lender. For instance the standard security might be held by a bank as a security for an overdraft. Is the bank really supposed to make a search in the

13 (1870) 9 M 252.

Personal Register every time a cheque is drawn on the account? To this difficulty there are several replies. The first is that it is the purpose of this work to state the law of inhibition, not to judge it. The second is that lending institutions are not the only parties to whom the law accords protection. To increase the protection of the bank is to reduce the protection of the inhibitor. It is not clear to the writer that the interests of the former should be favoured at the expense of the latter. The third reason is that the inconvenience to the bank should not be exaggerated. Personal searches are quick and cheap. Though it is not practicable to search every time a cheque is drawn, it is practicable to make a periodic search, especially when large sums are involved. The fourth reason is that it must be recollected that if there is an inhibition it does not follow that the bank has no security for the post-inhibition lending. The security is bad in a question with the inhibitor, but in a question with all other parties it is good. Reference is made to chapters 6, 7 and 8.

It should be further noted that an inhibition will not strike at the security in so far as it secures interest for pre-inhibition advances. Such interest is not a debt contracted after the inhibition (even though it accrues after the inhibition). See *Scottish Waggon Co v Hamilton's Trustee*[14] (1906). Likewise the inhibition will not affect post-inhibition lending if the lending is such as the creditor was obliged to make in terms of a pre-inhibition contract. This follows from first principles.

If the writer is correct in his view of the law, it is important to bear in mind the interaction of this rule with the so-called rule in *Clayton's Case*. By the latter rule credit entries on an overdraft account are ascribed against the earlier rather than later debit entries. Thus suppose that the overdraft stands at £50,000 and that the debtor is then inhibited. Subsequently there are further transactions on the account, with debits of £30,000 and credits of the same amount. In a question with the inhibitor the £30,000 credits will be deemed to be in reduction of the original £50,000. Thus for the purposes of the inhibition there will be £20,000 of pre-inhibition lending and £30,000 of post-inhibition lending. Accordingly if the bank is aware of an inhibition it should close the account and enter further transactions of a new account. (Assuming, that is to say, that it wishes to continue to provide credit at all.) Bankers are of course familiar with this method of neutralising the rule in *Clayton's Case*.

One last point on this whole question. As has been mentioned, the reason why inhibition did not affect subsequent lending in the old bond of cash credit and disposition in security was that there was statutory provision to that effect. But in *Campbell's Trustees*[15] (above) an additional ratio was suggested by Lord Jusice-Clerk Moncreiff. This was that 'if inhibiting creditors ... are to exclude the bank's security for advances subsequent to its date, so must all rights and diligences which would be preferable to the inhibition'. Such a result would indeed be absurd, but the learned Lord Justice-Clerk is (with respect) mistaken in supposing that such a result would ensue. His assumption of course is that the familiar vinco vincentem rule would operate. But the whole nature of inhibition ranking is calculated to circumvent the vinco vincentem rule. If A is preferred to B, and B by his inhibition is preferred to C, it does not follow that A is preferred to C. Reference is made to the Canons of Ranking and to chapters 6 and 7.

Although an inhibition will strike at future advances made on a pre-inhibition heritable security, it is thought that if, on default, the heritable creditor sells the security subjects, the purchaser's title will be unaffected by the inhibition. He is entitled to rely on the fact that the heritable security was granted before the inhibition, and is not under an obligation to enquire as to the timing of the advances made to the debtor. It is thought that in these circumstances the correct procedure for the inhibitor is to arrest in the hands of the selling creditor and then, failing settlement, to bring a furthcoming. In that furthcoming the post-inhibition advances will be treated as if they were unsecured. Naturally, in questions with non-inhibition creditors the post-inhibition advances are treated as secured, for the benefit of the inhibition is personal to the inhibitor. Much the same will apply, mutatis mutandis, if the inhibitor has adjudged before the sale.

Inhibition against creditor

We turn now to the less common case where the inhibition is against the creditor in the heritable security. Since a heritable security is itself a heritable right and since inhibition affects (subject to exceptions) all heritable rights, an inhibition by a creditor of the heritable creditor affects the security. This question falls to be considered under three heads, namely discharge, assignation, and sale.

Discharge

A heritable creditor is legally bound to grant a discharge upon payment

15 (1870) 9 M 252.

of the whole sum secured. Accordingly such a discharge is not the 'voluntary' act of the creditor. Hence it is not struck at by an inhibition against him.

If, however, the discharge is not such as the creditor was legally bound to grant (eg a gratuitous discharge) it will prima facie be in breach of the inhibition and so reducible. (Note, however, that the reduction, to be effective, may have to be within five years. See s 41 of the 1970 Act.)

The same rules likewise apply to restrictions of heritable securities.

The rules thus far are simple enough. But the waters are muddied by an Act of Sederunt of 19 February 1680 whereby if the inhibition is *notarially* certified to the *debtor* in the security, any further payments by him to the creditor are struck at by the inhibition. This AS was said to be still in force in *Macintosh's Trustees v Davidson and Garden*[16] (1898), though it was held not to cover the circumstances of that case. It is to be noted that in Alexander's edition of the Acts of Sederunt (1838), which purported to be a complete edition of all AS then in force, and which was published with the 'special approbation' of the Court of Session, this AS is omitted. The present writer expresses no view as to whether the AS is still good law. In practice it is a dead letter since such notarial certification is never used.

Assignation

An assignation of a heritable security by an inhibited creditor is struck at, provided of course that the assignation is not in implement of a pre-inhibition contract. (Cf *Low v Wedgwood*[17] (1814).) To this general rule there exists, however, an exception, namely where the assignation is tantamount to a discharge. For instance, suppose that the debtor wishes to switch his loan from one creditor (A) to another (B). He could do this by borrowing from B, in exchange for a security, and using the money to pay off A. Indeed, in modern conveyancing practice this is usually how this is done. But the alternative (which was formerly the usual method, and is still sometimes adopted) is for A to assign the security to B, with the amount of the loan passing directly from B to A. In *Mackintosh's Trustees*[18] (1898) it was held that such an assignation is not struck at by an inhibition against A since functionally it was merely an onerous discharge. Reflection will show that this exception is capable of swallowing up the rule, and there must be some slight doubt as to whether the

16 (1898) 25 R 554.
17 6 Dec 1814 Fac Coll.
18 (1898) 25 R 554.

case was correctly decided. In practice a law agent should hesitate before taking an assignation from an inhibited heritable creditor.

Sale

Though authority appears to be lacking, it is thought that a sale by a heritable creditor is struck at by an inhibition against him. If such a sale takes place the inhibitor can and should reduce it. Procedure thereafter is uncertain. In the opinion of the writer the inhibitor should then adjudge, not the security held by his debtor, which was extinguished by the sale, but the property itself. The position will then be that the property is owned by the purchaser, but subject to an adjudication. Personal liability will not be with the purchaser, but with the inhibitor's debtor, ie the former heritable creditor. The latter will be liable to the purchaser in warrandice.

Much the same will apply in the rarer case where title passes to the heritable creditor by decree of foreclosure. Though the decree will not be reducible, the inhibition will continue to be effective. The heritable creditor will then be in the position of any inhibited proprietor.

Different types of heritable security

This chapter has concerned itself with the standard security. Few of the older forms of heritable security are still in existence. The law is however, it is submitted, unitary, so that mutatis mutandis it makes little difference what species of heritable security is in question. It should be noted that the Act of 1970, which introduced the standard security, is silent as to inhibition. But that Act was not, and has never been interpreted as being, a self-contained code. The ordinary rules regulating the interaction of inhibition and heritable security must apply with equal force to the standard security.

CHAPTER 10

Bankruptcy

Scope of chapter

This chapter deals with the law of inhibition in relation to sequestration and to voluntary trusts for behoof of creditors. In general two issues arise. The first is whether an inhibition strikes at the title of the trustees and the second is as to the effect of the inhibition in the ranking. This chapter must be read in conjunction with the relevant parts of chapter 7.

Title of trustee in sequestration

Since the conveyance in favour of the trustee is a judicial one, it is probably the case on general principles that the title of the trustee does not constitute a contravention of any inhibition against the bankrupt. But it is necessary to appeal to general principles since s 31(2) of the 1985 Act expressly provides that the title of the trustee shall not be challengeable on the ground of any prior inhibition. Similar provision existed in s 97(2) and s 100 of the Bankruptcy (Scotland) Act 1913, and also in earlier legislation.

One small difficulty does, however, exist. The section states that the title is free from 'any' inhibition but does not state whether this means any inhibition against the bankrupt or, on the other hand, whether it also covers any inhibition against the bankrupt's author in title. For instance suppose that X when inhibited dispones to Y, and Y is soon thereafter sequestrated, what is the position in relation to the inhibitor? The Act of 1913 at s 97(2) uses the same phrase 'any inhibition' but at s 100 it speaks of 'any inhibition against the bankrupt' thus making it clear that the immunity is only in respect of inhibitions against the bankrupt. The opinion of the writer is that the immunity is only in relation to inhibitions against the bankrupt, and this for two reasons. In the first place it is improbable that there was any intention to change the law—indeed it is certain that there was no such intention. In the second place the interpretation here proposed is in conformity with the 'tantum et tale' rule. The trustee takes the estate of the bankrupt tantum et tale as it stood in the bankrupt. Consequently if the bankrupt's title was reducible ex capite inhibitionis then the trustee can acquire no better title than was vested in the bankrupt himself.

The immunity conferred by s 31(2) of the Act means that the trustee can sell the heritable property of the bankrupt without needing to obtain any discharge or recall of the inhibition, and, conversely, that a purchaser cannot object to the title offered on the ground of such inhibition.

Proceeds of sale

The rights of the inhibitor, such as they may be, are thus transferred from the subjects themselves to the proceeds of sale. Thus s 31(2) of the Bankruptcy Act, repeating the earlier legislation, when conferring immunity on the trustee, adds the words 'reserving any effect of such inhibition on ranking'.

The manner in which the inhibition is given effect to in the ranking is explained in chapter 7. In brief, the trustee must calculate two imaginary rounds. In the first round the inhibition is ignored, and the proceeds are allotted to the various creditors accordingly. In the second round the inhibitor 'draws back' from any post-inhibition parties such amount (and no more) as is necessary to put him into the position he would have been in had such parties not ranked. For instance, suppose that the inhibitor's debt is £6,000. Three months after the inhibition the debtor borrowed a further £30,000 from X. Three months later the debtor was sequestrated. The claims of the other creditors amount to £54,000. The heritage, after deduction of securities and the pro rata share of preferential claims, realises £30,000. At the first round all parties will get a dividend of 1/3, so the inhibitor will draw £2,000, while X will draw £10,000 and the others collectively will draw £18,000. Next, the trustee calculates what the inhibitor would have drawn had X not ranked. In that case the total claims would have been £60,000, so the dividend would have 1/2, so the inhibitor would have drawn £3,000. Therefore at the second round the inhibitor draws back £1,000 from X. The final ranking is thus £3,000 to the inhibitor, £9,000 to X and £18,000 to the other creditors.

It may be that the post-inhibition debt is secured. It is still of course subject to the inhibition. The following example will illustrate the ranking. The facts are as above, except that on making his loan X received a standard security. At the first round X receives £30,000. The inhibitor and other creditors receive nothing. At the second round the inhibitor draws back from X what he would have drawn had X not ranked. If X had not ranked the inhibitor would have drawn £3,000. The second and final round therefore gives the inhibitor £3,000, X £27,000, and the other creditors nothing.

It will be noted that in both this and the preceding example X's claim is good as against the non-inhibiting creditors, whose second round ranking is therefore the same as their first round ranking.

The leading case in this area is *Baird & Brown v Stirrat's Trustee*[1] (1872). On consulting this case it is advisable to consider the terms of the interlocutor pronounced as well as the judgments delivered.

In many cases an inhibition will have no effect whatsoever in the ranking. This will be so where there is no creditor claiming in the sequestration whose claim is founded on a post-inhibition debt or deed.

Preferential claims

There seems to be no direct authority, but there can be no doubt that the proper method of dealing with preferential claims is to ascribe them rateably as between heritage and moveables. An inhibitor is subject to such claims as are other unsecured creditors.

Moveables

Inhibition has of course no effect as against the moveable estate. But in sequestration the question arises as to whether the inhibitor must reckon the amount of his 'draw back' as being a security for the purposes of ranking against the moveable estate. The argument would be that in the first of the above examples the inhibitor must rank against the moveable estate not for £6,000 but only for £5,000 (£6,000 less the draw-back), while in the second example he would rank only for £3,000 (£6,000 less the draw-back). The law on this point is unclear, there being a conflict of judicial opinion, and general principles offering little guidance. The matter is discussed in chapter 7, where it is tentatively concluded that the better view is as expressed in *Scottish Waggon Co v Hamilton's Trustee*[2] (1906) namely that inhibition is not to be regarded as a security for these purposes.

It remains to be added that occasionally the question arises in relation to heritage also, in respect of heritage which for some reason is not affected by the inhibition.

Inhibition within 60 days

The 1985 Act makes one alteration in the old law, in relation to inhibitions effected within 60 days of the sequestration. This will be found at s 37(2) of the Act, which provides that

---

1 (1872) 10 M 414.
2 (1906) 13 SLT 779.

'no inhibition on the estate of the debtor which takes effect within the period of 60 days before the date of sequestration shall be effectual to create a preference for the inhibitor, and any relevant right of challenge shall, at the date of sequestration, vest in the permanent trustee, as shall any right of the inhibitor to receive payment for the discharge of the inhibition'.

The subsection goes on to make further consequential provisions.

Bound though the writer is to attempt an interpretation of this provision, he finds the task a difficult one. The subsection seems to have been conceived with the intention of bringing inhibition into line with poinding and arrestment, both of which are and always have been subject to a 60 day nullification rule. But the reason why poindings and inhibitions have been so regulated is that those diligences, if not so cut down, operate to give their users a preference over other creditors. Inhibition does not so operate, except in relation to parties whose claims arise after the inhibition and therefore with actual or constructive notice of it. An inhibitor, therefore, unlike a poinder or arrester, is not seeking to steal a march on anyone. In omitting inhibition from the 60 day rule the old lawyers thus had in mind the difference between that diligence and the others. The new provision thus appears to the writer to be a retrograde step, replacing good law with bad law. Naturally the writer hopes that in this opinion he is mistaken.

Inhibition has effect only if there are post-inhibition debts or deeds. Thus it is imagined that in the great majority of cases an inhibition within 60 days of sequestration will not strike at anything. Where this is the case the new provision will have no scope to operate.

The type of case in which it will apply will be where there is an inhibition, say, 50 days before sequestration, and, say, 10 days later there is a disposition or a standard security by the debtor. Take first the case of disposition.

Under the old law the disposition took the subjects out of the estate of the bankrupt, so that it was no concern of the trustee. The inhibitor would reduce and adjudge. The purchaser would normally purge the inhibition (or subsequent adjudication) by paying the inhibitor what he was due. This is still the pattern in the case of an inhibition more than 60 days before sequestration. Under the new law the inhibitor's 'right of challenge' is to 'vest' in the trustee. This form of words presents some difficulty. As has been emphasised elsewhere, the right to reduce is of little value unless it can be followed up by an adjudication. Yet the trustee, though he is given the inhibitor's power to reduce, is not given the inhibitor's power to adjudge. ('Right of challenge' is defined at s 37(3).) It may have been felt that this was unnecessary in view of the deemed adjudication in favour of the trustee under s 37(1) (a). But the position is unclear. Suppose that 50 days before sequestration the debtor is inhibited and that 10 days later he dispones property to X. It would seem that the deemed adjudication under s 37(1) (a) does not apply to this property at all, since at the date of sequestration it does not belong to the bankrupt. Under pre-1985 law the inhibitor could reduce and adjudge. Under post-1985 law the trustee can reduce, but his reduction is worthless unless he can also adjudge. The best guess is that the 'right challenge' is intended to include the right to adjudge after reduction.

In respect of what sum is the trustee to adjudge? Not, presumably, for the whole debts of the bankrupt. This would be to turn the low on its head. The general law is that a purchaser is free to buy property from an inhibited seller, if he is prepared to purge the inhibition by paying the sum due under the inhibition. It is inconceivable that the 1985 Act intended to change this rule. Therefore the trustee can adjudge only for the sum due to the inhibitor.

In practice of course a purchaser will usually not wait for a reduction and adjudication, but will voluntarily purge the inhibition by payment. The sum required for purgation will simply be the sum due to the inhibitor. Payment is to the trustee, not to the inhibitor, as s 37(2) itself makes clear. The trustee must, under the general law, give a formal discharge of the inhibition in exchange for this sum.

If the trustee does have to adjudge, things will be rather awkward, since an adjudication is generally rather slow to produce hard cash. But such problems do occasionally occur in sequestrations.

Assuming that X purges, what is the trustee to do with the money received? Section 37 gives no guidance on this, a little surprisingly. Presumably the trustee is not just to pay it over to the inhibitor, for that would be to make the whole rule rather pointless. Presumably, therefore, the money so received is simply to be added to the general fund available for the benefit of creditors. (Including both the inhibitor, and X himself.)

Where the deed is a standard security presumably much the same will apply, mutatis mutandis. The standard security holder must either give up his security or purge the inhibition by paying to the trustee the sum due to the inhibitor. Such sum will then be available to the creditors generally, including the standard security holder and the inhibitor.

The actual computation of this is, however, rather complex, and involves an additional round of ranking. (Yet another reason for doubting the wisdom of this innovation.) Take the second of the two examples given earlier in this chapter. Change only the dates, so that both the inhibition and the loan take place within 60 days of sequestration. Then the first two rounds are calculated as explained above. But the £3,000 allotted to the inhibitor is not paid to him. It becomes a fund for general distribution. The dividend on it will be 1/30. (Making the assumption that the dividend is to be calculated on the base-line claims. The Act is silent.) Thus the inhibitor will get £200, X will get £1,000 and the other creditors will get £800. The final result will therefore be that the inhibitor gets £200, X gets £28,000, and the other creditors get £1,800. In summary:

Party	Round 1	(ignore inhibition)
Inhibitor	—	
X	30 000	
Others	—	

Party	Round 2	(apply drawback)
Inhibitor	3,000	
X	27,000	
Others	—	

Party	Round 3	(distribute drawback to all parties pro rata)
Inhibitor	200	
X	28,000	
Others	1,800	

So far we have considered s 37(2) of the 1985 Act in relation to the first two effects of inhibition. (See chapter 6.) What of the third effect? Suppose for instance that 50 days before sequestration the debtor is inhibited and that ten days later he borrows money from another party?

One possibility is that s 37(2) is not meant to apply to the third effect of inhibition. This view would be based on the use of the word 'challenge' which might be taken to refer only to the procedure of reduction, which is not normally required in connection with the third effect (see chapter 8). But this seems a strained interpretation. Why should an inhibitor have the benefit of his inhibition if the post-inhibition creditor takes no standard security, but lose the benefit if he does take such a security? Why should the inhibitor's rights be invaded in one type of violation of the inhibition but not in another type? In the absence of clear language it must be supposed that Parliament intended the 60 day rule to apply generally.

It remains to illustrate the operation of s 37(2) in relation to the third effect of inhibition. Take the first of the two examples earlier in the chapter. Change the dates so that the inhibition is 50 days before the sequestration and the loan by X is 40 days before the sequestration. Section 37(2) has the effect of turning the two-round ranking into three rounds. For it is necessary to calculate the amount of the inhibitor's draw-back against X, and then, at the third round, to distribute that draw-back amongst the creditors generally (including the inhibitor and X).

The first two rounds are as in the first of the two examples given earlier in the chapter. This gave to the inhibitor a draw-back against X of £1,000. This now falls to be divided rateably between all parties. This yields (making the base-line assumption mentioned earlier) a dividend of 1/90. The final ranking is therefore:

Inhibitor	2,000 +	66.67 =	2,066.67
X	9,000 +	333.33 =	9,333.33
Others	18,000 +	600.00 =	18,600.00
			30,000.00

The author acknowledges that this is complex. Given the general complexity of inhibition ranking one would have expected any reform to have taken care not to increase the complexity. The innovation might have been justified by pressing necessity, but in the personal view of the writer not only was there no such necessity but it is even the case that the new provision has made the law less just.

Trust deeds

The remainder of the chapter will deal with voluntary trusts for behoof of creditors.

A voluntary trust deed for behoof of creditors is a voluntary future act and therefore is prima facie reducible by an inhibitor, so far as it relates to the heritable estate. (Cf Bell, 2,392.)

Whether such an inhibitor can actually reduce it depends on whether he has acceded to the trust deed. If he has acceded he is barred from reduction, for his accession constitutes a ratification of the conveyance to the trustee, and on first principles an inhibitor cannot reduce a conveyance which he has himself consented to. In the passage cited in the last paragraph Bell suggests that the inhibitor can reduce even after accession but it is submitted that this is incorrect for the reason here given. The only qualification to be made is that there are cases in which a creditor may resile from his accession, and of course if an inhibitor does so resile, and does so lawfully, then his right to reduce will re-emerge.

The 1985 Act introduces new provisions as to trust deeds which are relevant here. The Act (Schedule 5) provides that certain trust deeds will become 'protected'. Although the Act does not so express it (for the actual wording see para 6 of the Schedule) the effect of 'protection' is that all creditors are deemed to be acceding creditors. There can thus be no doubt that a non-acceding inhibitor cannot reduce a protected trust deed ex capite inhibitionis.

Assuming that there is no right of reduction the rights of the inhibitor, such as they are, are transferred to the proceeds of sale, as in a sequestration. Trust deeds invariably contain a clause stating that the estate is to be wound up as in a sequestration, so the voluntary trustee will in the ranking give effect to the inhibition accordingly, for which see above.

In practice the trustee should ensure that the inhibitor grants some form of discharge, for otherwise a purchaser may refuse to accept the title offered. (See chapter 12.) If the inhibitor refuses then the only practical solution may be for the trustee to petition for sequestration.

It remains to be added that in *Carlyle v Mathieson's Trustee*[3] (1739) it was held that once a trustee under a trust deed has carried out a sale, at a fair value, a non-acceding inhibitor cannot reduce. The ratio of this decision may be mora.

3 (1739) Mor 6971.

CHAPTER 11

Company law

Scope of chapter

This chapter considers inhibitions in relation to company law. The subject comes under four heads: floating charges, receivership, liquidation and administration.

As a preliminary remark it is necessary to say that company law has always been administered as part of English law, with a minimum (and sometimes less than a minimum) of adaptation for Scotland. (This has always been so, but a good recent example is given by the Insolvency Act 1985. The major alterations in Scots company law effected by this Act were introduced on the basis of consultation in England alone.) As a result it is not surprising that in not one of the four areas mentioned above is there any provision for the effect of inhibition, despite the fact that all four are purely the creatures of stature. This is in strong contrast with sequestration, which, since it has never dangled at the string of an English statute, has always had provision as to the effect of inhibition.

Floating charges

Floating charges were introduced by the Companies (Floating Charge (Scotland) Act 1961, later replaced by the Companies (Floating Charges and Receivers) (Scotland) Act 1972, which itself was replaced by Part XVIII of the Companies Act 1985. The charge is a quasi-security which can only be granted by corporate debtors and which is capable of covering all or part of the debtor company's property. (See generally s 462 of the Companies Act 1985.) It thus can, and usually does, cover the company's heritable property, which raises the question of its effect in relation to inhibition.

Ignoring for the moment the provision in the legislation about 'effectually executed diligence' (s 463 of the Companies Act 1985 and ss 55 and 60 of the 1986 Act), two propositions would naturally suggest themselves. The first is that a charge granted after the company is inhibited will be a violation of the inhibition quoad the heritable estate, on the general principle that inhibition bars the inhibited party from granting securities over immoveable property. The second proposition is that if the inhibition is laid on after the charge has been created then it will not strike at the charge, on the general principle that an inhibition strikes only at future acts. Thus what is relevant is the date of the charge, and not the later date when the charge attaches.

The writer is of the opinion that the view of the law presented in the last paragraph is not only the most plausible view, but is also the only correct one. But though there is no direct authority on the matter, this view is difficult to reconcile with *Lord Advocate v Royal Bank*[1] (1977) and *Armour and Mycroft Petitioners*[2] (1983). Behind these cases lies the provision in what are now s 463 of the Companies Act 1985 and ss 55 and 60 of the 1986 Act to the effect that when a charge attaches it is subject to the 'effectually executed diligence' of other creditors on the property in question. The first of the above cases held that an arrestment does not qualify under this provision. (The correctness of this decision, which was by a majority, has been much doubted. See further Sim 1984 SLT (News) 25.) The relevance of the case for present purposes is that it would seem that if an arrestment does not so qualify, then a fortiori an inhibition will not qualify either. In other words the implication would be that an inhibited company is free to grant a charge over its heritable property in disregard of the inhibition. This startling inference was duly drawn (albeit only obiter) in the second of the cases mentioned above.

It will be observed that both the 'natural' approach outlined earlier and this latter approach agree on one point, which is that an inhibition laid on after the creation of the charge does not strike at the charge. (Though they agree for different reasons. The 'natural' approach takes this view because the inhibition is too late. The 'unnatural' approach takes this view because it considers that inhibition is not an 'effectually executed diligence' on the property of the company.) Where the two approaches differ is concerning the less common case where the charge is created after the inhibition has been laid on. The 'natural' approach takes the view that the charge is struck at by the inhibition in relation to the heritable estate, while the other view takes the opposite position.

A full discussion of the meaning of 'effectually executed diligence' and the cases mentioned above would take up more space than the writer is willing to devote to it. The reader is referred to Mr Sim's article, above, and to the materials cited therein. The writer will restrict himself to making a single further point, namely that some of the weight of the decision in *Lord Advocate v Royal Bank*[1] rests on the ground that arrestment is not a diligence 'on' the property of a debtor company. (See in this connection an article at 1983 SLT (News) 177.) From this the inference was that a fortiori inhibition could not be a diligence 'on' the property of

1 1977 SC 155.
2 1983 SLT 453.

a debtor company. The 1985 Act however now expressly provides that inhibition is a diligence 'on' the estate of the debtor (see s 37(2)). (From which it now follows that an arrestment must also be a diligence 'on' the arrested property.) This is not to say that the choice of the word 'on' in s 37(2) of the 1985 Act has changed the law. Both arrestment and inhibition have always been considered as diligences in some sense 'on' the debtor's property (cf chapter 1). The choice of terms serves merely to re-assert a fact which, for various reasons, had been lost sight of in the *Royal Bank* case.

In conclusion therefore: (a) it is clear that a floating charge is not struck at by a subsequent inhibition; (b) there is no direct authority as to the effect of an inhibition on a subsequent charge; (c) on balance the better view appears to be that the inhibition will, in the case mentioned, strike at the charge so far as the charge covers property affected by the inhibition.

Given these conclusions, two further points require to be made. The first is that a charge, unlike an inhibition, affects acquirenda. Thus suppose that in Year 1, X Ltd is inhibited. X Ltd at that time own farm A. In Year 2, X Ltd grant a charge over their whole property and undertaking. In Year 3, X Ltd sell farm A and buy farm B with the proceeds. In that situation farm A is still subject to the inhibition, but not to the charge, while farm B is still subject to the charge but not to the inhibition.

The other point concerns the situation where the charge is prior to the inhibition (and thus not subject to it) but after the date of the inhibition the chargeholder makes further advances to the debtor company. This is essentially the same situation as was discussed in chapter 9 in relation to standard securities. In that chapter the conclusion arrived at was that an inhibition does strike at advances made by a creditor after the date of the inhibition. The same considerations apply in the case of floating charges. The post-inhibition advances made on the security of the charge will be subject to the inhibition in relation to the heritable estate affected by the inhibition.

Receivership

Receivership is one of the two means whereby a charge attaches (liquidation is the other). It was introduced in 1972 and is now governed, like charges, by ss 50–71 of the 1986 Act. The rights of the receiver will be subject to an inhibition to the extent that the charge on which he was appointed was so subject, but not otherwise. If the charge was granted after the granter was inhibited, the inhibitor will be able to reduce the charge and adjudge. The receiver will be unable to sell since the right of reduction and adjudication by the inhibitor would still be available after such sale. As a result the receiver will normally have to purge the inhibition by payment.

Where the charge is pre-inhibition, but post-inhibition advances have been made, the receiver is probably free to sell since a purchaser would appear to be protected under s 55(4) of the 1986 Act. What happens to the proceeds in this case is not clear. It is thought that the free proceeds (but before deduction of the chargeholder's claims) must be paid to the inhibitor (up to the amount of his debt). This would seem right on general principles and in addition can probably be spelt out of s 60 of the Act.

Section 61 of the 1986 Act (formerly s 477 of the Companies Act 1985 and previously s 21 of the 1972 Act) contains a provision which requires notice.

> 'Where the receiver ... is desirous of selling ... any property ... which is ... affected or attached by effectual diligence executed by any person; and the receiver is unable to obtain the consent of ... such person to such sale ... the receiver may apply to the court for authority to sell or dispose of the property ... free of such ... diligence. On such application ... the court may, if it thinks fit, authorise the sale ... free of such ... diligence ... on such terms or conditions as the court thinks fit.'

The reader is referred to the section for its full terms.

Considerable difficulties attend the interpretation of this section. It is not apparent what its precise meaning and effect are, nor to what types of situation it is supposed to apply. Moreover, it is surprising to find security rights and rights obtained by diligence subjected to discretionary provisions. Here it is not necessary, however, to consider the section generally but only in relation to inhibition. Where the inhibition is dated after the creation of the charge the inhibition will, as we have seen, not strike at the right of the receiver to sell the heritable estate. ('Inhibition in a question with them [pre-inhibition parties] has simply no effect at all.' Lord Mackenzie in *Scottish Waggon Co v Hamilton's Trustee*[3] (1906).) The section is therefore in this case not necessary. Notwithstanding, it was used in *Armour and Mycroft*[4] (above) in just this situation. Naturally, though such procedure is unnecessary, it is also harmless. The decision in question did, however, contain one error, in that it directed the receiver (or rather, in that case, the joint receivers) to pay any surplus that might emerge direct to the inhibitors. That decision was erroneous because it was at variance with the basic nature of inhibition. Inhibition is merely

3 (1906) 13 SLT 779.
4 1983 SLT 453.

a 'negative or prohibitory diligence' (Erskine, 2,11,13) and therefore 'the inhibitor has not ... without adjudication or other diligence any active title on which he can demand payment.' (Bell, 2,139.) Consequently the inhibitors had an active title to be paid only if they adjudged before the sale or arrested after it. The attention of the learned judge was not drawn to the Canons of Ranking. The interlocutor therefore was in disregard of the rights of other creditors. It must always be recollected that inhibition by its nature cannot prejudice the rights of pre-inhibition creditors. Not being parties to the process such creditors could therefore (it is respectfully submitted) reduce the interlocutor to the extent that it prejudiced their lawful claims. (See also chapter 8.)

The other case is where the receivership proceeds upon a charge which is post-inhibition. In that case the inhibition does strike at the right of receiver to sell such estate as is affected by the inhibition. Whether s 61 of the 1986 Act would be relevant in this type of case, and if so how, is not clear to the writer. Much could be said on this question, but for brevity the writer merely offers his tentative opinion that the section could indeed be resorted to and that that proper course for the Court to take would be to authorise the sale on condition that the receiver pay the proceeds (after deduction of expenses and real securities) in the first instance to the inhibitor, up to the value of his debt, the chargeholder receiving any remaining balance. At first sight this procedure might seem objectionable for the same reasons outlined earlier in connection with *Armour and Mycroft* but it is submitted that such a view would be superficial. Very briefly the inhibitor is entitled to payment since he alone of the creditors can object to the sale. (The position is thus, at a deep level, similar to the leading case of *McLure v Baird*[5] (1807), discussed in chapter 8.)

It will be observed that a sale by a receiver is very similar, as far as inhibitions are concerned, to a sale by a heritable creditor. (See chapter 9.)

Liquidation

Parliament has never made any provision as to the effect of inhibition in liquidation, whether voluntary or compulsory. This fact may seem surprising given that such provision has always been included in the successive Bankruptcy (Scotland) Acts. The explanation doubtless lies in the attitude of the Department of Trade and Industry and its predecessors (whose responsibility Scots commercial legislation is).

5 19 Nov 1807 Fac Coll.

The background: before 1986

It may be best to begin by explaining the development of the problem prior to 1986.

(1) As already stated, successive statutes dealing with liquidation failed to make any provision for the effect of inhibition. (This, as will be seen, continues to be the case.)

(2) The first notice of the problem is in Stewart. Stewart (p 567) said that in a compulsory liquidation an inhibition had the same effect as in a sequestration. His argument was that a compulsory liquidation gives a deemed decree of adjudication. This argument seems rather precarious. There is no general rule that an adjudger takes free from an inhibition. (Sometimes he does, and sometimes not.) Stewart does not discuss voluntary liquidation. (But see p 745.) In his day (unlike the present) a voluntary liquidation did not give a deemed decree of adjudication. Stewart devotes very little space to the matter.

(3) Next, Burns raised the question. He reached a different conclusion. He argued that Parliament had expressly provided that in sequestrations an inhibition would not stop the trustee from selling, but had chosen to make no such provision with reference to liquidation. The inference must be that a liquidator did not take free from inhibition. This argument applied to all kinds of liquidation. The passage will be found at p 294 of the 3rd edition (1926), the last by Burns himself, and stands substantially unchanged in the 4th edition (1957), pp 300–301. Between the two editions there was the Companies Act 1948, which once again declined to adopt the rule applicable in sequestrations. As with Stewart, Burns does not give the question more than a couple of sentences.

(4) The present writer examined the question at length at 1984 SLT (News) 145. I questioned Stewart's argument. Quite unpardonably I failed to discover what Burns had said. I concluded that both compulsory and voluntary liquidations were in the same position as sequestrations, essentially for two reasons. The first was a policy argument. Liquidations would not be able to function properly if the law was not so. The second was a technical argument. A compulsory liquidator had the same general powers as a trustee in sequestration. (Section 245(5) of the Companies Act 1948.) A voluntary liquidator had the same general powers as a compulsory one. (Section 303(1) (b) of the same Act.) Since a trustee in sequestration had power under the Bankruptcy (Scotland) Act 1913 (and previous Acts) to sell free from inhibition, the same must be true of compulsory and voluntary liquidators.

(5) The Companies Act 1985 and the Bankruptcy (Scotland) Act 1985 made no changes requiring notice for present purposes, with one

exception (affecting Stewart's argument), namely that the deemed decree of adjudication was no longer in favour of the liquidator, but directly in favour of the creditors. See s 37(1) of the latter Act, applied to liquidations at first by Sch 7, para 21. (Now s 185 of the 1986 Act.)

(6) The matter was then dealt with by Professor J. M. Halliday in the second volume of his *Conveyancing Law and Practice*. Though this was published in 1986, it appeared before the 1986 Act. At p 361 he deals with the matter very briefly. He says that liquidation is in the same position as sequestration, and as authority cites the Bankruptcy (Scotland) Act 1985, Sch 7, para 21. This paragraph of the 1985 Act (which, as was mentioned above, has since been repealed but re-enacted as s 185 of the 1986 Act) deals with the effect of liquidation (both compulsory and voluntary) upon antecedent diligence. It does not mention inhibition at all, except in relation to the comparatively minor matter of inhibition within 60 days of liquidation. This provision is, however, the successor (subject to one or two changes) of the statutory provision upon which Stewart had founded his argument. On the other hand Professor Halliday neither cites Stewart nor states Stewart's argument. (Nor does he mention the opinion of Burns.) Thus Professor Halliday's position is not quite clear.

The 1986 developments

The Insolvency Act 1986 repealed the previous legislation. The present law is thus to be found partly in that Act and partly in statutory instruments made under it. The most important of these for present purposes is, at the time of writing, the Insolvency (Scotland) Rules 1986 (SI 1986 1915).

Though the 1986 Act was essentially a consolidating measure, it made two changes which are significant for present purposes. The first is that the rule that voluntary liquidators have the same general powers as compulsory ones has been repealed and not replaced. (This rule, in the last period of its existence, was to be found in s 598(2) of the Companies Act 1985.) The second is that for the first time it is possible for the Secretary of State to provide, by Order, that particular provisions of the Bankruptcy (Scotland) Act 1985 are to apply to liquidations. (This innovation is hidden away in Sch 8, para 14 of the 1986 Act.) The 1986 Rules do not adopt that provisions of the Bankruptcy (Scotland) Act as to inhibitions.

Assessment of the post-1986 Law

The 1986 legislation has added great strength to the argument of Burns. Prior to 1986 there was at least a case to be made that the omission of a provision similar to that found in the successive bankruptcy statutes was simply inadvertent, a result of mere neglect. But it is difficult to see how that 1986 legislation can be given the benefit of these pleas. Whereas in 1948 (the previous opportunity for change) inhibition against companies was very uncommon, by 1986 it had become an everyday problem. If it was intended that inhibition should have the same affect as it does in sequestration, it is very hard to believe that this would not have been incorporated into the 1986 legislation. This point receives further support by the new provision, mentioned above, whereby any rule within the 1985 Act can now be, by Order, extended to liquidation. The Secretary of State was thus given the option to extend the sequestration rule. The decision was not to extend it.

The foregoing paragraph applies to all kinds of liquidation. The next point concerns only voluntary liquidations. (Which in practice means creditors' voluntary, since in members' voluntary the company will normally be solvent.) As has been mentioned, the 1986 Act repealed the provision whereby voluntary liquidators had the same general powers as compulsory liquidators. Yet this provision was, in the writer's view, the sole technical means whereby such a liquidator could sell free from inhibition.

Conclusions

Where does all this leave us? With great uncertainty. With some hesitancy the current position may be summarised as follows:

(1) The policy argument in favour of the sequestration type of rule is still valid, for what it is worth.
(2) The Stewart argument is, it is submitted, even more precarious than it used to be. The reason is that whereas under the older law a liquidator had in his favour a deemed decree of adjudication, this is no longer so, the deemed decree being in favour of the various creditors individually. This point may also be relevant to Professor Halliday's position, depending upon what his precise position is. Furthermore, and really quite fatally, it would seem, for this whole line of argument, a simple *decree* of adjudication is of little value unless and until the adjudger is *infeft* upon the decree. (See chapter 13.)
(3) The technical argument based on liquidators' powers still applies to compulsory liquidations. It no longer applies to voluntary liquidations. (Liquidations under the supervision of the Court have, of course, been abolished.)
(4) The argument of Burns, which is that the sequestration-type rule does not apply in any type of case, has been immeasurably strengthened.

(5) Voluntary liquidation is the voluntary act of the company and therefore *prima facie* subject to inhibition.

A purely personal assessment would be that on a bare balance of probabilities compulsory liquidation has the same effect as sequestration in relation to inhibition, while the opposite applies to voluntary liquidations, but again on a bare balance of probabilities.

Where a company is inhibited, therefore, it may be advisable to choose a compulsory liquidation rather than a voluntary one, and if the latter has already begun it may be advisable to convert under s 116 of the 1986 Act. However the problem in many cases may disappear where there is a heritable security or a concurrent receivership, for which see the next sections.

The conveyancing implications are discussed in the next chapter.

Liquidation and heritable security

In practice the heritage will very often be subject to a standard security. That may materially affect the situation. Paragraph 4.22 of the Insolvency (Scotland) Rules 1986 applies to liquidation the provisions of s 39(4) of the 1985 Act, which regulate sale when there exists heritably secured debt. The liquidator may sell without the consent of the heritable creditor(s) only if enough is realised to pay them in full. Otherwise he must sell with their consent.

Provided that the liquidator sells with their consent (which may still be asked for even if not required under s 39(4)) then it is thought that the title conferred on the purchaser will be free from any inhibition against the company. The reason is that a standard security holder has power to sell free from inhibition, and this power must logically also cover a sale by a liquidator to which the standard holder is a party. But this proposition is subject to two qualifications. The first is that it presupposes that the standard security was created prior to the inhibition. If this is not the case the standard security will normally be subject to the inhibition, with the result that the holder cannot confer on the liquidator any power of sale. The other qualification, purely practical, is that the standard security holder should either be a co-grantor of the need or at least execute concurrence on it.

Liquidation and floating charges

If there is a floating charge then it is likely that any liquidation will either be preceded by or accompanied by a receivership, for which see above. In a majority of cases it would seem that the receiver can sell free of inhibition.

Ranking

Where the sale can be effected free of the inhibition there can be little doubt that the inhibitor falls to be ranked upon the proceeds of sale according to the general law applicable.

Inhibition within 60 days of liquidation

The provisions of s 37(2) of the 1985 (inhibition within 60 days of sequestration) are applied to liquidation (both compulsory and voluntary) by s 185(1) (a) of the 1986 Act. Reference is made to the last chapter as to the meaning and effect of these provisions, with regard to ranking. With regard to the question of the power of the liquidator to sell, the inference would appear to be that a liquidator, even voluntary, is able to sell free from any inhibition within the 60 days.

Administration

Administration is a new company insolvency process introduced by the Insolvency Act 1985 and now regulated by the 1986 Act. It was introduced into Scottish company law without any serious attempt at consultation, so it is perhaps not surprising that there is no clear guidance as to how it is supposed to interact with the law of inhibition.

Sections 10 and 11 of the 1986 Act have a general provision that creditors cannot use diligence after an administration order is made, and, in addition, that this effect draws back to the date of the presenting of the petition. It is therefore clear that inhibition from this date is incompetent. However, one or two particular points require consideration. First, what if there is inhibition while the petition is depending, but the petition is thereafter dismissed? In that case the terms of s 10 lead to the conclusion that the dismissal does not validate the inhibition. Re-inhibition will be required. If this is correct, however, it leads to injustice, since in practice the inhibiting creditor will not be aware, in most cases, that there ever was such a petition, for the petition is not noted either with the Registrar of Companies or in the Personal Register. Thus he may have an inhibition which is ex facie valid, which he bona fide believes to be valid, which ought in equity to be valid, and which will be believed to be valid by third parties, but which is latently invalid. This being the case, it must be a possibility that the Court of Session will exercise its equitable powers so as to give to s 10 a non literal reading, in the event that the petition is dismissed.

Secondly, what if, before the petition, the creditor has obtained warrant to inhibit, and perhaps has served the inhibition, but has not registered in the Personal Register? Will such registration become incompetent as a result of the presenting of an administration petition?

The answer depends on how s 10 and s 11 are to be read. The view of the writer is that the registration would become incompetent.

Thirdly, there is the case of the creditor who has registered a Notice of Inhibition before the petition but who then finds that a petition has been presented before he can register the inhibition itself. Once again it appears to the writer that ss 10 and 11 make such registration incompetent. As a result the Notice will lapse after 21 days.

In all these cases it should be noted that the Keeper of the Registers will not normally know that an administration order has been made, or a petition presented. The inhibition will thus appear on the Personal Register in the ordinary way, competent or incompetent.

It remains to add that the provision in the Insolvency Act as to public notice of administration proceedings are most unsatisfactory. There is no notice at any stage in the Personal Register. The Register of Companies is notified once the order has been made, but the administration has up to 14 days to do this, an extraordinary length of time. But, even worse, the effect of the order operates from the date of the petition. Thus for a period of indefinite length—it may be considerable— diligence is invalidated, though creditors, sheriff officers and messengers-at-arms, and indeed courts other than the court hearing the petition, will be unaware that the steps they are taking are invalidated. This is bound to cause both injustice and technical complications.

The other issue is the effect of administration on inhibitions already executed and registered against the company. Sections 10 and 11 of the 1986 Act provide that diligence may not be 'continued'. This will mean, for instance, that a poinding cannot be completed by warrant sale, or arrestment by furthcoming. But it is thought that it will not mean that an inhibition will cease to have effect. Once an inhibition is registered it is complete. There is nothing to be 'continued'. There is therefore nothing in these two sections to rob an existing inhibition of its effect.

What if the administrator wishes to sell property subject to such an inhibition? Section 15 has provisions whereby if an administrator wishes to sell property which is subject to a 'security' he may do so subject to certain conditions. Except in the case where the security is a floating charge, there are two such conditions: (1) He must obtain the leave of the court. (2) The proceeds of sale must be applied in the first instance towards paying the secured creditors according to their lawful ranking. Unfortunately it is unclear whether an inhibition is a 'security' for the purposes of s 15. The term 'security' is defined in s 248. The definition is a very wide one, and, indeed, very similar to the definitions of the same word to be found in the successive Bankruptcy (Scotland) Acts. However, as was mentioned in chapter 7, it is uncertain even in bankruptcy law whether inhibition counts as a 'security'. It is therefore doubly uncertain whether it so counts for the purposes of the 1986 Act. Furthermore in ss 10 and 11 the concepts of security and of diligence appear to be contrasted. On balance, and having regard to the general tenor of s 15, the writer is of the view that inhibition is not a 'security' is the relevant sense.

If this conclusion, however, is wrong, the inhibitor is in a very strong position, for on such sale he will be paid in full. (Or at least up to the value of the subjects sold, after deduction of such ordinary securities, such as standard securities, as are not themselves struck at by the inhibition.)

Another reason for supposing that inhibition is not a 'security' for the purpose of s 15 is that where the inhibition was on the dependence a very odd result would ensue. Section 15 would require the inhibitor to be paid, even though his action might at the end of the day be unsuccessful. It is difficult to believe that this is what was intended.

We are therefore left with the following conclusions. (1) Inhibition which was already in existence is not invalidated by sections 10 and 11. (2) Inhibition is not a 'security' for the purposes of s 34. What then happens if the administrator wishes to sell property subject to inhibition? The net result must be that the inhibition would strike at any such sale. The company is thus in the same position that it was in before the administration proceedings began. Unless it can find a purchaser who is willing to take a title subject to inhibition (very unlikely) no sale will be possible unless the inhibition can be discharged. Where the inhibition is in execution this will in practice mean that the inhibitor will have to be paid in full. Where the inhibition is on the dependence, there will have to be payment, or caution, or consignation, according to the general rules as to getting rid of any inhibition on the dependence. (See chapter 3.)

CHAPTER 12

Conveyancing practice

Scope of chapter

The object of this chapter is to attempt to state good conveyancing practice in relation to inhibitions, and generally to consider inhibitions from the viewpoint of the working conveyancer. Inevitably it is not self-contained, but to a large extent presupposes the exposition in the other chapters.

Constitutive entries in the Personal Register

The entries in the Personal Register constituting an inhibition are either (a) letters of inhibition or (b) summons with warrant to inhibit. Also possible is (c) certified copy interlocutor granting motion to inhibit, but this is rarely seen in practice.

Frequently seen is the notice of inhibition (usually though not necessarily in the form of notice of letters of inhibition). This constitutes an inhibition but only if within 21 days it is followed up by an entry as stated in the previous paragraph. If not so followed up, it is without effect. If followed up outwith the 21 day period the inhibition takes effect only as from the second entry. See further s 155 of the 1868 Act. Accordingly if the search reveals a notice of inhibition but nothing else, and 21 days have elapsed, the search is clear. Nevertheless in such circumstances the conveyancer should be on the qui vive since the existence of such a notice makes it likely that an inhibition will soon make its appearance.

Three other entries require notice, which, though they are not inhibitions, take effect more or less as inhibitions.

(1) Notices of litigiosity. There are three types of notice of litigiosity. (a) The notice of summons of reduction. This is put on the Register on the dependence of an action of reduction. (b) Notice of summons of adjudication, which is registered on the dependence of an action of adjudication. (c) Notice of rectification under s 8(7) of the Law Reform (Miscellaneous Provisions) (Scotland) Act 1985. This is registered on the dependence of an action to rectify a deed. The effect of a notice of litigiosity is the same as that of an inhibition,

with one difference, namely that its effect is restricted to the property in question, and does not extend to other subjects. The first two types of notice of litigiosity are regulated by the 1868 Act, s 159, the 1924 Act, s 44, and the Law Reform (Miscellaneous Provisions) (Scotland) Act 1985, Sch 2, paras 4 and 5. The third type is regulated by s 8(8) of the last mentioned Act. The latter regulations seem to be substantially the same as the former, except that they appear to make no provision as to prescription.

(2) Sequestration notices. As soon as a petition for sequestration is made, the clerk of court must register in the Personal Register a notice to that effect: s 14 of the Bankruptcy (Scotland) Act 1985. This operates as an inhibition against the debtor. It should be observed that this procedure applies only in the case of sequestration and not in the cases of liquidation or receivership or administration.

(3) Trust deed notices. Under Sch 5, para 2 of the Bankruptcy (Scotland) Act 1985, the trustee under a voluntary trust deed for behoof of creditors may register in the Personal Register a notice which has the effect of an inhibition against the truster. Presumably the inhibition operates for behoof of all the creditors. The trustee is not obliged to adopt this procedure, but it is thought that in practice he would be unwise to omit it.

Extinctive entries in the Personal Register

The discharge of an inhibition may be either voluntary or judicial. In either case it may be either total or partial, a partial discharge being one which restricts the effect of inhibition to certain subjects while leaving it in force as against others.

Judicial discharge is of three forms. The first is decree of recall. The second is interlocutor of recall. The third is decree of dismissal or decree of absolvitor, in cases where inhibition was used on the dependence of an action, but the action has been unsuccessful. In such a case it is competent simply to extract the decree in favour of the defender and to record it, this of itself extinguishing the inhibition.

In the case of a registered certified copy interlocutor of recall there exists a danger which requires notice. In theory it is possible for such interlocutor to find its way on to the Personal Register even though there has subsequently been a successful reclaiming motion against the interlocutor. The author has, however, never encountered a case in which this has actually happened. If it did happen, it is unclear whether a party bona fide relying on the faith of the registers would be protected.

Occasionally an inhibition will be wholly or partially extinguished by a decree of declarator or of reduction. In such a case the extract decree can be recorded in the Personal Register.

Length of search

Inhibition prescribes in five years: s 44(3) (a) of the 1924 Act. As a result the practice is not to search further back than five years from the date of the close of the search, on the principle that any inhibition prior to that time will be defunct. There does, however, exist a difficulty here, discussed in chapter 3. On the one hand it is clear that any transaction entered into by an inhibited party after the inhibition has prescribed will be unchallengeable. But on the other hand it is not quite certain that the prescription of the inhibition operates retro so as to validate a transaction effected prior to prescription. An example will illustrate the problem. In Year 1, A inhibits B. In Year 4, B dispones to C. In Year 7, C sells to D. If D's law agent searches back just five years, to Year 2, he will not discover the inhibition. This does not matter if we presume that the right to reduce the disposition by B to C prescribed at the same time as the inhibition itself, ie in Year 6. But is this presumption correct? Might the law not be that the right to reduce a contravention of the inhibition prescribes not at the same time as the inhibition itself, but independently?

Usually what happens of course is that there is not a new search but merely a continuation of an existing search. In the example just given, D's law agent will see from the existing search that B was inhibited when he disponed to C. What he makes of that discovery will depend on what view he takes of the difficulty here discussed.

The decision is one that must be taken by the law agent himself. If he is satisfied that violations of inhibitions cease to be reducible five years after the date of the inhibition, then he will be satisfied with instructing a five-year search, or, where there is an existing search, he will disregard entries more than five years old. This approach has the sanction of custom. On the other hand if he feels, like the author, that there exists an element of doubt, he should, theoretically, insist on a longer search. How long? The right to reduce a violation would, on this view, probably prescribe twenty years after the date of the violation. Alternatively it would be possible to appeal to positive prescription, which would in normal cases cure the defect more swiftly. Accordingly the rule would be that the length of search should be the shorter of (a) twenty-five years (twenty years of long negative prescription plus a further five years) or (b) back to the date of the foundation writ (ie the last conveyance prior to a date ten years back).

If the law agent takes this latter approach, what should he do if he finds that a conveyance forming part of the prescriptive progress was reducible? In such a case he should consider the title offered to be unacceptable. There is of course some risk here either way. If he accepts the title he runs a risk that it is reducible. If he rejects it he runs the risk that the seller will seek damages for breach of contract, on the ground that the title was good. The conveyancer who wishes to take this approach should therefore frame the missives acccordingly.

Where the subjects are on the Land Register, the problem, already difficult enough, becomes even worse. Reference is made to chapter 2. The 1979 Act requires the Keeper to enter on the Title Sheet adverse entries in the Personal Register, but this is a duty which, for reasons explained in that chapter, cannot always be carried out, and there is deep uncertainty as to what is the effect of an omission.

Parties to be searched against

The last section was concerned solely with the question of the length of search. The question now for consideration is as to which parties need to be searched against.

In general the rule can be stated as being that a party must be searched against if he held an adjudgeable interest in the property, since inhibition strikes at such rights as could be adjudged. (See chapter 4.) Thus inhibition, like adjudication, strikes at what might loosely be called beneficial interest. Infeftment is not the criterion. Thus suppose that A dies and bequeathes property to B. B does not complete title but sells to C, the disposition being granted by A's executor with the concurrence of B. In that case C should search against B. Or again, suppose that title is in the name of D, but D holds as nominee for E. E sells to F, the disposition being granted by D. F must search against E. In each of these cases the real seller is different from the party who grants the disposition, and in each case it seems clear that the real seller holds an adjudgeable interest.

Occasionally it can happen that neither the titles nor other circumstances known to the purchaser will indicate the identity of the party beneficially entitled. For instance a party purchasing from a nominee may be unaware that he is a nominee, so that a search against the real seller is impossible. In such a case there can be little doubt that an inhibition against the real seller will be of no effect as against such a purchaser. The test is good faith.

In the cases mentioned above the question will also arise as to whether the nominal seller should be searched against. The case of the executor is discussed later in this chapter. As for the nominee, he is a species of trustee, for which again see later in the chapter. The question of search against other types of seller such as the liquidator of a company are also discussed later.

A situation which often arises is where the seller, or some earlier party, has held the subjects only on missives. Is it necessary to search against such a party? The traditional practice has been that parties holding subjects on missives should be searched against. As against this the case

of *Leeds Permanent Building Society v Aitken Malone and Mackay*[1] (1986) held
that the right of a purchaser under missives is a moveable right and thus
not affectable by inhibition. This case is discussed in chapter 4, where it
was suggested that its correctness is not beyond doubt. Given the
existence of this doubt the only safe course is to adhere to the traditional
practice. (See also the discussion of inhibition against a purchaser later
in this chapter.) It therefore seems advisable that offers to purchase
should stipulate that the personal search is to be extended to parties who
have held the property only on missives.

Designation

It is obviously of importance that the Memorandum of Search fully
identifies the parties to be searched against, for otherwise relevant
inhibitions may not be disclosed. For instance the seller must be
identified not only by his current address but by all other addresses
which he may now have or has had within the previous five years. Thus
a professional person will often have two addresses, one being his home
address and the other being his business address. Both addresses must be
given, since an inhibition may design the inhibited party by either
address. The agent for the purchaser is here very much in the hands of
the agent of the seller. Consequently the agent for the seller should
ensure that he obtains the necessary information from his client, and
transmits this to the other agent. It is thought that this is a matter of
professional ethics, but it is possible that it goes further than this. It may
be that an agent for a seller who does not take reasonable care to provide
full information for making up the Memorandum would be liable in
delict.

Where a party is being searched against in a representative capacity,
such as an executor, this should be made clear in the Memorandum.

Having identified the parties to be searched against in terms of the
quality of their interest, it remains to identify them in terms of the
period when their interest was held. It might seem, in view of the five
year prescription, that it is only necessary to search against parties who
have held 'proprietorial' interest within the preceding five years. But the
position is not so simple, for two reasons. One is the difficulty mentioned
above, namely that an inhibition more than five years old may still be
relevant in so far as the prescriptive progress depends on a deed which
was granted at a time when the inhibition was still in force. The other
reason concerns sequestration notices under s 14 of the Bankruptcy
(Scotland) Act 1985 (formerly s 44 of the 1913 Act). Such notices have
the effect of inhibition, but unlike actual inhibitions they can be

1 1986 SLT 338.

protected from prescription by re-registration. For example suppose that A was sequestrated in Year 1 and in Year 3 disponed to B. (This of course is unlikely. It presupposes that the trustee has not taken over the property, that A is fraudulent, and that B is prepared to take a bad title.) In Year 9, B sells to C. If C's law agent takes the view that there is no need to search against A since A has had no interest in the property within the previous five years, he will be mistaken. In Year 9 the original deemed inhibition will still be alive, provided that A's trustee has duly kept it alive by the renewal procedure provided in s 14 of the new Act. (Under the old Act the renewal had to be every five years. This is now reduced to every three years.)

Hence the traditional advice, to be found in the textbooks, is that search should be made against all parties who have had a 'proprietorial interest' in the subjects within the period of positive prescription. Where (as is usually the case) there is an existing search the law agent should check the earlier entries accordingly.

Example

In 1959, A disponed to B. In 1969, B disponed to C. In 1979, C disponed to E with the consent of D. It is now 1987 and E has concluded missives to sell to F. Against whom should F's law agent search against? He should search against all parties who have had a 'proprietorial interest' within the period of positive prescription. The foundation writ is the first conveyance prior to ten years before 1987, ie is the deed of 1969, so all parties with such an interest since 1969 must be searched against. B, C, D and E must all therefore be included.

Having identified the parties, how far back should the search be made? The conventional rule that it should be made only five years back from the date of search, ie in the example back to 1982.

But the counsel of perfection is to make it longer than this, on account of the difficulty discussed earlier in the chapter. Suppose that C had been inhibited in 1978. This fact would not show up in a search back only to 1982. On one view of the law the inhibitor's right to reduce the disposition of 1979 prescribed in 1983. But the alternative possibility is that it does not prescribe till either 20 years have passed (1999) or till the title is secure by positive prescription (1989), whichever is the earlier. So the only course which is strictly safe (though it is not done in practice) is to search back to the foundation writ (1969) or 25 years (1962) whichever is the later (1969). Such a search would show up the inhibition against C in 1978, the effect of which may be that the 1979 disposition is still (1987) reducible.

In the usual case the law agent will have before him an existing search which will provide much of the necessary information. In the example given, it is probable that in 1979 a search was made against C (and D) back to 1974. This will have picked up the inhibition against C. In practice of course it is unlikely that E would in those circumstances have proceeded with the purchase at all.

Where the subjects are on the Land Register, and there is no exclusion of indemnity, the search should (as a counsel of perfection) be carried back 25 years in every cases, since for such property the potentially shorter period of positive prescription will be of no assistance. Paradoxically in this respect titles which have an exclusion of indemnity are better protected. (See the 1979 Act s 10, modifying s 1 of the Prescription and Limitation of Actions (Scotland) Act 1973. There can be no doubt that the drafting of s 10 was defective, the paradox in the text being merely one example. But the subject cannot be entered into here.)

'Clear search'

Missives usually stipulate for a 'good and marketable title' and also that there shall be delivered or exhibited 'clear searches' in the relevant registers. If a letter of obligation is granted, as is usually the case, it generally undertakes that the search will disclose no 'deed or diligence' prejudicial to the title. The question of whether a search satisfies these requirements in any particular case is often one of some difficulty.

It is necessary to make a distinction between the terms 'good' and 'marketable'. A title is good if in fact it is valid and unchallengeable. A title is marketable if from the deeds and searches it appears that it is good. Thus a title may be (a) good and marketable, or (b) good but not marketable, or (c) marketable but not good, or (d) neither good nor marketable. Most titles fall under (a). An example of (b) would be where the seller is inhibited but the inhibition turns out to be invalid for some reason. An example of (c) would be where a deed in the prescriptive progress is forged, though this fact is not apparent. Titles which are not only bad but obviously so fall under (d).

The reason why an obligation is given to provide a title which is not only good but also 'marketable' is partly that a buyer does not wish to purchase litigation, even if it promises to be successful litigation, and partly that when he comes to sell he does not wish to have difficulties with the law agents for the new purchaser.

It is thought that an obligation to provide 'clear searches' is an obligation to produce searches which will show a marketable title. The leading case here (though not in all respects a perfectly satisfactory one) is *Dryburgh v Gordon*[2] 1896). (See also *Duke of Devonshire v Fletcher*[3] (1874).) Here a seller had been inhibited while title stood in the name of his creditor under an ex facie absolute disposition. The disposition in favour

2 (1896) 24 R 1.
3 (1874) 1 R 1056.

of the purchaser was granted by both the debtor (substantive owner) and the creditor (formal owner). The purchaser later sued the firm of agents acting for the seller under their letter of obligation. The defence was that the title was good since the inhibition was ineffective. In truth of course the opposite was the case: the sale was indeed struck at by the inhibition. This was the basis of the decision by the Lord Ordinary. The Second Division adhered, but on the more general ground that whether the inhibition was effective or not, its existence in the circumstances was a breach of the obligation to produce clear searches. In other words, whether the title was good or bad, it was not marketable.

Although the general principle is well settled, it is difficult to say in particular cases when an inhibition, though it does not make the title bad, nevertheless makes it unmarketable. On this *Dryburgh* offers little guidance, for in the circumstances of the case the inhibition did in fact make the title bad. There are agents who seem to take the view that any inhibition making its appearance on the search will render the title unmarketable, however obvious it may be that the inhibition is without effect. Fortunately such agents are few. Here are some examples where the entries in the Personal Register would not prevent the search from being regarded as clear:

(a) There was an inhibition against the seller, but it was more than five years before the present sale.
(b) There is a notice of inhibition. But more than 21 days have elapsed and there is no other entry.
(c) There was an inhibition but the search discloses that it has been discharged or recalled.
(d) There is an inhibition but its date of registration is after the date when the purchaser completed title.
(e) The proprietor was inhibited after the registration of a standard security in favour of the creditor who, after default, is now selling under his power of sale.
(f) The proprietor was inhibited but was thereafter sequestrated and the subjects are now being sold by the trustee.

This is not an exhaustive list, but merely enumerates certain cases where the law seems too clear to be doubted.

The opposite state of affairs is where though the inhibition is ineffectual the practice is to regard the title as unmarketable, or, in other words, the search not clear. The example arising most commonly in practice is where the seller is inhibited after concluding missives but before title has passed to the purchaser.

It is now necessary to consider various particular cases where the conveyancer will require to decide, firstly whether the title is good, and secondly, if it is good, whether it is marketable.

(1) Inhibition after missives

A very common case is where the seller is inhibited after the conclusion of missives but before title has passed to the purchaser by registration. It is well settled that in this case the inhibition does not strike at the sale, for it is too late. So the title is good. Settled conveyancing practice is, however, to regard the title as unmarketable. See *Henderson v Dawson*[4] (1895) per Lord McLaren. This common situation is further discussed later in this chapter.

(2) Standard securities

Under this head, reference is made to chapter 9. For present purposes standard securities fall to be discussed from two aspects: where there is a discharge, and where there is a sale by the heritable creditor.

It is not the practice to search against the heritable creditor who has granted a discharge. This is because in general a discharge of a heritable security is not the sort of deed which could be challenged by an inhibitor of the creditor. This practice is safe enough, but the conveyancer should be aware of two possible sources of danger. One is where the discharge is gratuitous. This is very rare, of course. But the law is that a gratuitous discharge is reducible by an inhibitor of the heritable creditor. The other point arises from the Act of Sederunt of 19 February 1680. This makes a discharge, even for full value, reducible, but only if the inhibition, in addition to other requisites, has been *notarially* served on the debtor in the security. It is an open question whether this AS is still in force. But even if it is the danger is fanciful since notarial service is never used.

Additional protection is afforded by the fact that in general discharges more than five years old cannot be reduced: s 41 of the 1970 Act.

Where the heritable creditor is selling the security subjects in virtue of his power of sale, he must be searched against personally, since the law appears to be that an inhibition against him will strike at the sale. Search against the debtor in the security, in the case of sale by the heritable creditor, need only be made in respect of the period before the creation of the security. The reason is that an inhibition against the debtor before he granted the security will normally render the security reducible (and so strike at an eventual sale by the heritable creditor), while an inhibition against the debtor after the security has been granted will not affect the heritable creditor since, at the relevant date, the granting of the security was not a future act.

4 (1895) 22 R 895.

What if part of the sums secured by the security were advanced to the debtor after the date of the inhibition? In chapter 9 the view was expressed that in such a case the inhibition strikes at such advances. But it is thought that this is a matter between the inhibitor and the heritable creditor and does not affect a purchaser from the heritable creditor. As far as the purchaser is concerned, all he need check is that the heritable security in virtue of which the sale is being carried out was created before the date of the inhibition.

Sequestration

Reference is made to chapter 10. The 1985 Act, s 31(2), expressly provides that the title of the trustee is free from any inhibition against the bankrupt. So no such inhibition can be objected to by a purchaser. Such inhibitions therefore do not require to be searched for. Nor is it necessary to search against the trustee in sequestration. In his capacity as trustee acting under judicial authority he cannot, it is thought, be inhibited, while any inhibition against him as an individual would be irrelevant.

(3) Trust deeds

Reference is again made to chapter 10. The statutory protection which exists for sequestration does not exist for voluntary trusts for creditors. If the debtor was inhibited then prima facie the conveyance by him to the trustee is reducible quoad the heritage. Accordingly a title offered by the trustee would not be marketable and would probably even be reducible. The purchaser should therefore insist on a search against the debtor.

If the inhibitor has acceded to the trust then he is barred from a reduction. In that case the title offered by the trustee is good. But nevertheless the purchaser's agent should not regard the search as clear. He should insist on a registered discharge or restriction. From the point of view of the trustee, he should, before sale, check the Personal Register, and he should be careful not to conclude missives of sale unless he is sure that any relevant inhibition will be discharged or restricted by the inhibitor. If the inhibitor proves stubborn, the only safe course is to convert to a sequestration.

It should be noted that under the 1985 Act if the voluntary trust becomes 'protected' then all the creditors are deemed to be acceding creditors. In that case the title offered by the trustees will be 'good' but the author still tentatively suggests that without discharge or restriction the search will not be clear. It is open to argument, however, whether such a view might not be too conservative.

It is advisable to instruct a search against the trustee, in his capacity as trustee, since in theory a case could arise in which a disgruntled creditor might obtain inhibition against him.

(4) Liquidation

Reference is made to chapter 11, where it is argued that there is great uncertainty as to the power of a liquidator to sell free from an inhibition against the company.

The writer's personal view is that on the one hand a purchaser should accept such a title from a liquidator, but, on the other hand, he should do so only if he is given a personal indemnity by the liquidator against the inhibition. This should be stipulated for the missives. If the liquidator does in law have the power to sell free from inhibition then such an indemnity will not affect the liquidator. If on the other hand such power does not exist, the purchaser, who has paid a fair price, deserves such protection. The indemnity should of course be in probative form, and it should make clear that the liquidator is bound not merely as liquidator, but personally also.

The difficulty will not arise if the liquidator can persuade the inhibitor to grant a discharge.

If there exists a standard security over the subjects, and the standard security holder has consented to the sale, and is to execute his concurrence on the disposition, then no indemnity is needed. This, however, holds good only if the security is ranked before the inhibition. Whether this is so can easily be ascertained from a search.

(5) Receivership

Again, reference is made to chapter 11. Given the poor quality of the statutory provisions concerning floating charges generally it is not surprising that there is no guidance as to the effect of inhibition. On the question of whether the title offered by the receiver is good or bad, the law appears to be (though this might be controverted) that if the floating charge on which the receivership proceeds was granted before the date of the inhibition, then the charge prevails over the inhibition, so that a purchaser is protected, but in the less common case where the charge is granted after the date of the inhibition the charge is struck at by the inhibition (to the extent of the heritage held by the company at the date of the inhibition and included in the charge).

Accordingly the purchaser's agents should require a search against the company, and should refuse the title if the charge was granted after the company was inhibited.

Assuming that the charge was pre-inhibition, the title is good, but it may be questioned whether the search can count as 'clear'. The author's opinion is that it is clear. But the same advice here must be offered as in certain other cases. To forestall difficulties the missives and letter of obligation should be duly qualified.

A search against the receiver is probably unnecessary, since it is difficult to see how there could be any valid inhibition against him in his capacity as such. The writer would nevertheless require such a search on the principle of safety first.

(6) Administrators

For administrators appointed under the 1986 Act, see chapter 11. Inhibitions laid on after an administration order is made, or while a petition for such an order is depending, are ineffectual. Notwithstanding this, the view could be taken that in such a case the title offered by the administrator, while good, is not marketable, since the search will not appear to be clear. The law agent for the administrator should therefore ensure that the missives and letter of obligation are so framed that the purchaser cannot take an objection on this ground.

As for inhibitions already laid on, the conclusion in chapter 11 was (a) that they are not invalidated by sections 10 and 11 of the Act and (b) that they are not 'securities' for the purposes of s 15. Therefore a purchaser from an administrator would take subject to such inhibitions. Such a purchaser should therefore decline to accept such a title unless and until such inhibitions are discharged.

(7) Partnerships

Reference is made to chapter 5. The partnership should be searched against under its firm name. It is common to add a search against the partners as individuals, but this seems unnecessary. In the eyes of the law the firm and its partners are separate persons.

(8) Trusts

When taking a title from a trust the trustees should be searched against as such (except in the case of a trustee in sequestration). They need not be searched against as individuals.

In some cases it will also be necessary to search against one or more beneficiaries. The test is whether the consent of the beneficiary was necessary to the sale. If it was necessary, then an inhibition against the beneficiary may strike at the sale. If no such consent was necessary, no search against a beneficiary is necessary.

In cases of inter vivos trusts it may also be necessary to search against the truster, depending on how long ago the trust was set up.

(9) Executries

Reference is made to chapters 3 and 5. The question of whether an inhibition against a party now deceased will strike against a conveyance by his executor is an open one. The conclusion of the writer is that it probably does not. But the motto of the conveyancer is 'ob majorem cautelam' and so a party taking title from an executor should require a search against the defunct and should decline to settle if there is an undischarged inhibition. It follows that an executor would be unwise to conclude missives before ensuring that there is no inhibition registered against the defunct.

The executor is a trustee and accordingly need not be searched against personally. But he should be searched against in his capacity as executor, since it is possible for the creditors of the defunct to inhibit him as such.

It is also sometimes advisable to search against one or more of the beneficiaries of the estate. For instance suppose that the sale is of a house which has been bequeathed to X. X does not wish to take the house itself but asks the executor to sell it and remit the proceeds. In such a case an inhibition against X is liable to strike at the sale. The test here is the same as for trusts in general, for which see above, namely that if the sale by the executor requires the consent of a beneficiary then that beneficiary must be searched against, but if the executor may sell without any such consent then no search is required.

The advice given in the foregoing paragraph is not always adhered to in practice. Normally the risk involved is small. Naturally an inhibition against a beneficiary before the death of the defunct is irrelevant since at that stage the property is acquirenda in relation to the beneficiary.

Section 17 of the Succession (Scotland) Act 1964 gives no protection in this kind of case.

(10) Occupancy rights

Where a sale is by an entitled spouse and the non-entitled spouse has occupancy rights under the Matrimonial Homes (Family Protection) (Scotland) Act 1981, the sale will require either a discharge of those rights or a consent to dealing. In neither case is it necessary to search against the non-entitled spouse, since occupancy rights cannot be affected by inhibition. (See chapter 5.)

Inhibition during transaction

It commonly happens that a seller is inhibited after missives have been concluded but before settlement. It is well settled that in such a case the inhibition is too late to stop the sale, so that if the purchaser simply ignores the inhibition and settles the transaction, he is safe. In other words the title offered is good. But it is equally well established that the title is not 'marketable' so that the purchaser can refuse to settle standing the inhibition. What course of action should the agent for the purchaser actually adopt? There are a number of possibilities.

The first is simply to settle and to put the missives up with the titles, the missives constituting the evidence that the sale was a post-inhibition transaction. Though in theory this is safe, there are three practical dangers. One is that the inhibitor may raise an action of reduction. Such an action can be resisted successfully, but a purchaser does not wish to be involved in litigation, even if it is to be successful. The second danger is that when the purchaser comes to resell, the agent for the new purchaser will take a less relaxed attitude, and demand that the inhibition be discharged. The third is that by the law of evidence missives which are adopted as holograph do not prove their own date. As a result, this course of action is seldom taken in practice. See further *Henderson v Dawson*[5] (1895) per Lord McLaren.

A second possibility is the same as above, but to raise an action against the seller to clear the search. Alternatively the action may be against the seller's agents on the basis of the letter of obligation (as happened in *Dryburgh v Gordon* (1896)). A variation on this is for the purchaser to raise an action against the inhibitor for declarator that the inhibition does not strike at his title. Such a declarator when obtained can be registered in the Personal Register. Once again, this possibility is not often adopted in practice.

A third possibility is simply to refuse to settle. This is perhaps the most commonly adopted possibility. Much depends on the stage at which the inhibition is discovered. If it is discovered at an early stage, the seller has a sporting chance of clearing the title, and in addition the purchaser has reasonable warning that he may not get entry. But if it is discovered at the last minute, there is little chance of getting rid of the inhibition in time, and the consequences to the purchaser of not getting entry may be serious. His furniture may already be in the lorry. It should be added, at a more general level, that there may be some risk involved in postponing settlement. For if the inhibition against the seller proves to be a prelude to bankruptcy, delay may cause the purchaser considerable practical difficulty and may even lose him the purchase.

A fourth possibility is to take entry without payment of the full price. This is quite common. There is more than one variant. One is to consign the price in joint names. Another is to pay the price less a retention equal to the amount claimed by the inhibitor. This possibility naturally requires the consent of the seller, which is usually, but not always, forthcoming.

It need hardly be said that the purchaser's agent should keep his client informed of developments.

Future advances

Reference is made to chapters 9 and 11. The problem here is where the agent is acting for a lender who holds security for all sums due and to become due, and it is desired to make further advances. The security may be by way either of standard security or by way of floating charge (assuming that the charge covers heritage, as it normally does). In the opinion of the author an inhibition registered after the creation of the security or charge will strike at future advances (assuming that they are not advances already contracted for). Accordingly the only safe course to take is to make a new personal search against the borrower before the new advance is released. This is not always done in practice. Very often the risk is negligible. Thus, suppose that a householder of good financial standing with a building society loan of £20,000 over his £60,000 house wishes to borrow a further £3,000 to modernise his kitchen. Here there would be little risk involved in omitting a personal search. But in cases where the security is not so good, or the borrower is of more doubtful standing, or larger sums are involved, the conveyancer would be unwise to omit a personal search.

Where the security or charge secures an overdraft account, it would clearly be unworkable to carry out a personal search every time a new cheque is drawn on the account. If the sums involved are small it is probably not worth taking any action, but where more substantial sums are involved it is advisable to make a regular check of the Personal Register.

Letters of obligation

The agents for the seller should beware of granting, and the agents for the buyer should beware of accepting, an undertaking to deliver a discharge of an inhibition by a third party. The reason is that it is not normally within the power of the seller's agents to ensure that such a discharge is delivered.

Adjudication

Little needs to be said about adjudication in the context of conveyancing practice. The main warning to be given is that, notwithstanding the wording of s 62 (as amended) of the 1868 Act (which is analysed in chapter 13), an adjudication does not give the adjudger a title of ownership, unless and until a declarator of expiry of the legal has been obtained. The writer is aware that cases have occurred in practice where purchasers have accepted a title from an adjudger in ignorance of this fact. On the other hand it is competent to purchase an adjudication. This is done by assignation duly recorded in the Sasine Register or duly registered in the Land Register. An adjudication is, during the legal, much like any other heritable security, and can thus be assigned in much the same way.

Warrandice

Normally the question of inhibition and warrandice will not arise, for the purchaser will have inspected the interim report on the Search and will refuse to settle if there is disclosed any effectual inhibition. Alternatively, it will very occasionally happen that a purchaser will agree to take a title subject to an inhibition. For instance this might happen if the purchaser were willing to pay off the inhibitor himself. If this is the agreement, it should of course be provided for in the missives. In this connection the danger should be borne in mind that the missives will be superseded by the disposition, so it is necessary to make provision that the missives will not be so superseded.

It does, however, occasionally happen that a purchaser finds that his title is subject to an effectual inhibition for which he has not bargained. In that case the question arises as to whether the existence of the inhibition constitutes a contravention of the warrandice which will almost certainly have been granted in the disposition. The difficulty here is that the authorities on warrandice state that a seller cannot be sued under warrandice unless and until 'eviction' has taken place. It is one of the problems of the law of warrandice that what counts as 'eviction' is a matter of some uncertainty. The word itself suggests actual dispossession, but the case law shows that this is not always required. There can be no doubt that if the inhibitor has brought a successful action of reduction against the purchaser's title then there will be 'eviction' and warrandice is incurred. But it is uncertain whether inhibition on its own will count. The only case in which the question has been raised seems to be *Frendraught v Balvenie*[6] (1624). For warrandice generally, and particularly the problem of eviction, see K. G. C. Reid's contribution to *A Scots*

6 (1624) Mor 16575.

Conveyancing Miscellany: Essays in Honour of Professor J. M. Halliday (1987) (ed. D. J. Cusine).

Standing the unsatisfactory state of the law of warrandice it is difficult to give confident guidance on this matter. The tentative view of the writer is that the inhibition of itself will not ground an action in warrandice. Nevertheless it is suggested that the purchaser can protect his position by paying the inhibitor what he is due and then suing the seller under warrandice, on the basis that the payment, which was necessary to protect the title, constituted an eviction. If the inhibition is only on the dependence, such payment will be inappropriate. In that case it is thought that the purchaser can petition for recall, himself consigning in court the sum in respect of which the inhibition was used. He can then sue the seller as above. It must, however, be stressed that the suggestions in this paragraph are speculative only.

Inhibition against the purchaser

It sometimes happens that a purchaser is inhibited at or about the time of purchase. This does not stop the transaction, which may proceed as normal. But there may be consequences for a heritable creditor of the purchaser, and for a sub-purchaser. Two questions arise for decision. (1) Is the property to be classified, in relation to the inhibition, as acquirenda or as acquisata? If the former, the inhibition does not affect the property: it is non-inhibited estate. If the latter, the property is affected by the inhibition. Reference is made to chapter 4, where it will be seen that doubt exists as to what is the correct tempus inspiciendi. The traditional view is that property is acquisata as soon as missives have been concluded. But in *Leeds Permanent Building Society v Aitken Malone and Mackay*[7] (1985) it was held that the relevant moment is the delivery of the disposition. It is possible that this decision is not correct. It may be that the traditional view is correct, and it may even be that the correct tempus inspiciendi is the date when the purchaser acquires a real right. The advice to agents acting for heritable creditors and sub-purchasers must therefore be that they should not take it for granted that property is acquirenda unless the inhibition pre-dated the conclusion of missives. It may be that they will be ready to rely on the *Leeds* case, but they should be aware that there may be some risk in doing so.

The second issue (2) is that even if the property is affected by the inhibition it may be that the creditor or sub-purchaser is protected by reason of having a prior personal right. Take for instance the following sequence of events. On 1 June A concludes missives to purchase

7 1986 SLT 338.

property. On 15 June he accepts a formal offer of loan. On 7 July the loan cheque is requisitioned. On 11 July the transaction is settled and the disposition delivered. On 12 July A is inhibited. On 14 July the disposition and standard security are registered in the Land Register. In these circumstances it is probably the case that the property is affected by the inhibition. But nevertheless the security is protected from the inhibition because the purchaser came under a binding obligation to grant it before the date when he was inhibited. (In other words, the granting of the security was not a 'future voluntary act' in the relevant sense.)

Example of personal search

I conclude this chapter with an example of a personal search, followed by some comments. It should be noted that different firms of searchers present the information in very slightly different ways.

SEARCH in the REGISTER OF INHIBITIONS AND ADJUDICATIONS

against

ZYKKZYN LIMITED

from 29 December 1981
to   28 December 1986

30 December 1981. Letters of Inhibition, Siegfried Danziger, 25 Foster Park Gardens, Jedburgh:—against ZYKKZYN LIMITED, 1 Golden Square, Cupar, Fife.

21 April 1983. Notice of Letters of Inhibition, Orkney Map Co Ltd:—against ZYKKZYN LIMITED 1 Golden Square, Cupar. Signeted 17 April 1983.

24 April 1983. Letters of Inhibition, Orkney Map Co Ltd:—against ZYKKZYN LIMITED 1 Golden Square, Cupar.

25 March 1986. Notice of Letters of Inhibition, Robert Sutherland, 36 Lidderdale Street, Kirkcudbright:—against ZYKKZYN LIMITED, 1 Golden Square, Cupar, Fife. Signeted 24 March 1985.

24 April 1986. Letters of Inhibition, Robert Sutherland, 36 Lidderdale Street, Kircudbright:—against ZYKKZYN LIMITED, 1 Golden Square, Cupar, Fife.

6 May 1986. Notice of Letters of Inhibition, Lloyds Bank PLC:—against ZYKKZYN LIMITED, 1 Golden Square, Cupar. Signeted 1 May 1985.

22 May 1986. Notice of Summons and Inhibition, Governor and Co of Bank of Scotland:—against ZYKKZYN LIMITED, 1 Golden Square, Cupar, Fife. Signeted 20 May 1986.

28 May 1985. Discharge by Orkney Map Co Ltd of Inhibition (registered 24 April 1983) against ZYKKZYN LIMITED, 1 Golden Square, Cupar.

1 June 1986. Summons and Inhibition, Governor and Co of Bank of Scotland: against ZYKKZYN LIMITED, 1 Golden Square, Cupar.

22 July 1986. Letters of Inhibition, Oxford Book Co Ltd:—against ZYKKZYN LIMITED, 1 Golden Square, Cupar, Fife.

Searched in the Register of Inhibitions and Adjudications and found as above. [Signed on behalf of searchers.]

Danziger's inhibition is now (1987) prescribed. If it were the only entry on the search, the search would be clear.

The inhibition by the Orkney Map Co has been discharged. We do not know the reason for the discharge, but this does not matter.

Sutherland's inhibition takes effect as from 24 April. The Notice which he recorded in March is without effect, because not followed up within 21 days.

Lloyds Bank have no inhibition at all.

The Bank of Scotland have an inhibition which is operative as from 22 May. This is because the effect of inhibition is backdated to the date of the Notice is registered within 21 days of the Notice.

The Oxford Book Co have an inhibition effective from 22 July. The fact that they did not first record a Notice does not matter.

The search reveals that the inhibition of the Bank of Scotland is on the dependence of an action in the Court of Session. But no inference is possible about the other inhibitions. They may be either in the Court of Session or in the Sheriff Court, and they may be either on the dependence of an action or in execution.

CHAPTER 13

Adjudication

Scope of chapter and introductory remarks

This chapter gives a summary of the somewhat archaic law of adjudication as it exists in modern law. Such a treatment is necessary, for although adjudication and inhibition are two separate diligences, the law of inhibition presupposes the possibility of following up the inhibition with adjudication, and if it were not for the existence of that possibility inhibition would lose its value. In practice it is often sufficient for the inhibitor to rely on the possibility of adjudication without actually adjudging. As so often in law, the mere threat of adopting a compulsitor renders the actual use of the compulsitor unnecessary.

Adjudication is uncommon in current practice. The author has no statistics, but would guess that in a typical year there are fewer than twenty adjudications brought to decree. This contrasts sharply with earlier practice. For instance in the mid nineteenth century, when the number of heritable proprietors was far less than at present, adjudications were being brought to decree at the rate of about two hundred a year. (See *Parker on Adjudication*, preface.) This decline correlates with the increase in the use of inhibition, which is curious, for one would expect a rise in the use of inhibition would automatically lead to a rise in the use of adjudication. It is even stranger when it is considered that, subject to certain qualifications, adjudication is a much more powerful diligence than inhibition.

The general impression among law agents and counsel is that adjudication is slow, cumbrous, archaic and obscure. Consequently most do not resort to it. The process is self-reinforcing, for by being unfamiliar, it is not used, and by being unused, it is unfamiliar. This is unfortunate. Adjudication is in some ways unsatisfactory, but is nevertheless an extremely powerful weapon available to the unpaid creditor and, in the interests of their clients, agents should employ it more than they do. As, for difficulty, it is in fact a very easy diligence to use in practice. As for slowness, it usually proceeds swiftly, for in the great majority of cases the action is not defended.

Adjudication does have certain archaic features. The Scottish Law

Commission, as part of their general programme on the law of diligence, are likely, within the next few years, to make recommendations which will remove these features and make this diligence better adapted to modern practice.

Since the present chapter seeks to give only the rudiments of the law of adjudication, concerning which there is little room for controversy or doubt, citation of authority will be sparse. Readers who require further information on points of detail are referred to Stewart, to *Parker on Adjudication*, and to the standard texts on Court of Session procedure.

General nature

Adjudication proceeds by court action, and is directed at specified heritable property. The extracted decree is then registered in the Sasine Register or Land Register. The effect then is to give the creditor a judicial heritable security over the subjects. This entitles him to remove the debtor and lease the subjects, taking the rents towards his debt. The debtor can redeem at any time. If after ten years the debt is still unpaid, the creditor can convert his security into a title of absolute property by the special action of declarator of 'expiry of the legal'.

Procedure

The action is exclusively a Court of Session process. The summons specifies the property to be adjudged, and should identify it by a sufficient conveyancing description, for otherwise the creditor will be unable to register his decree, which would render it worthless. For property registered in the Land Register this will mean including the reference number of the property. The ground of action will normally be a decree for payment against the debtor, which of course must be condescended upon. A decree of registration is of course also sufficient. It is also competent to adjudge on a liquid document of debt, though this is not common. The document is only liquid if the debt is already due and resting owing. If the creditor holds a document of debt which is not yet liquid (eg a promissory note not yet matured) he can still adjudge in security, for which see below. If the creditor holds no decree or liquid document, he may raise a combined action of constitution and adjudication, but this is rare.

In practice the creditor will normally already have inhibited, but it is not necessary that he should have done so, since inhibition and adjudication are separate diligences.

Notice of litigiosity

There is more than one sort of notice of litigiosity. Here we are concerned with such a notice on the dependence of an action of adjudication, commonly called a notice of summons of adjudication. The creditor will normally register such a notice at the commencement of his action, but is not obliged to do so. He would, however, be unwise to omit to do this. The notice is registered under the name of the debtor. It has the effect of an inhibition against him, but only in relation to the property which is the subject of the action. The notice must identify the subjects in question. Probably a conveyancing description is necessary. In the case of property in the Land Register this will involve giving the number of the title sheet. Notices of litigiosity are regulated by the 1868 Act, s 159, the 1924 Act, s 44 and the Law Reform (Miscellaneous Provisions) (Scotland) Act 1985, Sch 2, paras 4 and 5. The latter operate by amending the 1868 Act. It was the new Act which first introduced the requirement that the subjects be identified in the notice, a useful reform. For further details the reader should refer to these various enactments.

Course of action

The action proceeds substantially as other Court of Session actions. Reference is made to the standard texts on Court of Session procedure. One speciality, however, which requires notice concerns intimation to other creditors. At first calling an interlocutor is pronounced by the Lord Ordinary which orders intimation in the Minute Book and on the Walls. The purpose is to enable other creditors of the debtor to know that an action of adjudication has been raised, so that they may take appropriate steps themselves. They are entitled to be conjoined as pursuers, though this does not happen often.

Extract and abbreviate

On obtaining decree the creditor can obtain either an extract or an 'abbreviate' of the decree, or both. The former is necessary for registration in the Sasine Register and Land Register and the latter for registration in the Personal Register. (Except where what is adjudged is itself a heritable security. In that case the creditor may register in the Sasine or Land Register either an extract or an abbreviate, as he chooses. See s 129 of the 1868 Act.) Since various changes in the law have meant that registration in the Personal Register is seldom necessary, abbreviates are seldom necessary.

Completion of title

Just as a disposition, or a heritable security, does not give the grantee a real right merely by delivery, but requires registration, so an extracted decree of adjudication does not give the adjudger a real right. He must complete title, like any other grantee of a heritable right. He does this in the same way as for any other heritable right, namely by registration in the Sasine or Land Register, according to whether the subjects adjudged are themselves registered in the one register or the other. For sasine property the extract will naturally require to have the usual warrant added and signed by the adjudger's law agent.

Where the adjudication is of a property on the new register, it is the practice for the Keeper to insert the adjudger's name in the Proprietorship Section of the Title Sheet, without deleting the name of the debtor. He also notes the adjudication in the Charges Section. (See the Registration of Title Practice Handbook at D.4.13.) In an article at 1983 JR 177, the present writer criticised this practice as illogical, on the ground that the debtor and the adjudger were not co-owners or joint owners. I would now withdraw this criticism and apologise accordingly. If (as was indeed argued in that very article) an adjudication operates as a double title, the first as an infeftment in security and the second as an infeftment in fee, subject to a suspensive condition, the practice is a perfectly logical one.

Unregistered property

In certain cases the property adjudged is not registered in the Sasine or Land Register. Some leases for instance fell into this category. In such cases the adjudger completes title by recording his decree in the Personal Register.

Stamp duty

The question of stamp duty on adjudications is potentially a matter of obscurity, but in practice the opinion of Burns can be accepted (p 534) that the decree is exempt from stamp duty, while the declarator of expiry of the legal falls to be stamped either at the value of the debt or at the value of the property, whichever is less. If the adjudger acquires absolute title by prescription he will escape stamp duty altogether.

Expenses

The position as to expenses is not entirely clear. Reference is made to Stewart p 589 and to MacLaren on Expenses pp 109–110. See also *Riley v Cameron*[1] (1940).

Effect

An adjudication is judicial heritable security. Accordingly it is an infeftment in security and not in fee, ie it does not divest the debtor of

---

1 1940 SLT (Sh Ct) 42.

his title. The debtor continues to be sole heritable proprietor of the subjects. The position of the adjudger is thus similar to that of a standard security holder who is in possession.

When enacting s 9 of the 1970 Act, which sought to abolish all existing forms of heritable security, to prepare the way for the new form, the standard security, Parliament overlooked the fact that adjudication was also a heritable security. There can be little doubt that an adjudication satisfies the definition of 'heritable security' given in s 9(8) (a), the reference to 'disposition' in that paragraph being met by s 62 of the 1868 Act (as amended by s 62 of the 1874 Act) which provides that an adjudication is to be considered as a disposition for statutory purposes (see below). If the view is taken that unambiguous statutory provisions must be given effect to, the necessary conclusion is that adjudication ceased to be competent in 1970. But as it happened, no one noticed this accidental abolition, and adjudication continued in use. Indeed, Parliament has itself assumed the continuing competence of adjudication in such enactments as s 31(1) (b) and s 37(1) (a) of the 1985 Act and s 12 of the Matrimonial Homes (Family Protection) (Scotland) Act 1981. However unambiguous, s 9 of the 1970 Act cannot be taken literally. Adjudication continues to be competent.

Section 62 of the 1868 Act (as amended by s 62 of the 1874 Act) provides that an adjudication is to be deemed to be a 'conveyance in ordinary form'. At first sight this looks as if an adjudication operates as an actual transfer of the property (ie an infeftment in fee) with merely a personal right of redemption in the debtor. (This would mean that the creditor would be in a position rather like that of a creditor in the now superseded ex facie absolute disposition.) But this would be a misinterpretation. Some technical conveyancing knowledge is required here. 'Conveyance' is defined in s 3 of the 1868 Act as including adjudications and heritable securities. The word is therefore neutral as to whether the adjudger is infeft in security or infeft as of fee. The old law therefore survives, namely that it gives an infeftment in security. The purpose of s 62 (and here one must admire the technical skill of the draftsman) is to link up adjudication with s 15 of the Act. Prior to the Act the mode in which an adjudger completed title was cumbrous in the extreme. After extracting the decree he had to charge the superior for entry. The superior then issued him a charter of adjudication. This contained precept of sasine. The adjudger then executed the precept by taking sasine, and then obtained from the notary an instrument of sasine, narrating the charter. He then registered the instrument. It was only at this final step (exhausted, and the poorer for his legal fees), which could take months and even sometimes years (especially if, as sometimes happened, the dominium directum was in non-entry), that the adjudger was infeft in his adjudication, with a real right in the subjects. The procedure was thus akin to the procedure for completing title in the ordinary case. The radical (and wholesome) reform effected by the mild nineteenth century conveyancing statutes was to sweep away this rigmarole and replace it by a system in which the grantee completed title simply by direct registration of his deed. The draftsman had to ensure that the new system applied to adjudgers as to other heritable grantees. The key section of the 1868 Act for this purpose was s 15, and to link up with s 15 it was necessary to state that an adjudication is deemed to be a 'conveyance'. All this was perfectly familiar to the conveyancers of the last century, but is naturally not so well known today, when feudal conveyancing is no more than a harmless pastime for eccentrics.

The writer has been reluctant to go into this digression, but it is necessary to do so in order to avoid the misunderstandings that s 62 can otherwise cause. Thus s 62 has often been transcribed into textbooks without comment, and in at least one case (*Gibson v Hunter Home Designs Ltd*[2] (1976)), it has found its way from the textbooks into a Court of Session judgment. The danger is that simple repetition of the statutory words without explanation almost inevitably will lead to misinterpretation. The two points to emphasise are that an adjudication leads to infeftment in security not infeftment in fee, and that the decree itself does not give that infeftment, but merely enables the adjudger to complete title in the ordinary form.

An additional purpose of this digression is to explain why it is that the Personal Register bears the name of the Register of Inhibitions and Adjudications, seeing that adjudications are not normally registered in it. There are two reasons. One is unconnected with the foregoing, namely that in certain minor cases adjudications can only be registered in the Personal Register. The other explanation is that because at common law it took so long for an adjudger to complete title, registration in the Personal Register was allowed as an interim measure which would be effectual for certain purposes connected with ranking. (See below.) This use of the Personal Register, though still competent, is no longer necessary, since title can be completed almost at once under the Acts of 1868, 1874 and 1979.

Unrecorded titles

There are two exceptions to the rule that an adjudication is non-divisitive. The first of these is where the property in question is not held on a recorded or registered title, for instance certain types of lease. In such a case the property is transferred to the adjudger, subject only to a personal right of redemption in the debtor. The second case is where the property is registered but the debtor is uninfeft. A typical example

2 1976 SC 23.

would be where the debtor has taken the property by succession by means of a docket under the Succession (Scotland) Act 1964, and has not completed title. In such a case also the effect of the adjudication is to give the adjudger a title of property subject only to a personal right of redemption. His position is then similar to the position of the creditor under an ex facie absolute disposition.

In such cases completion of title by the adjudger is different from the normal case. In the first of the cases just mentioned, the procedure is for the adjudger to complete title by registering the abbreviate of adjudication in the Personal Register. In the second of the cases the procedure is to complete title by Notice of Title or Notarial Instrument. The deduction of title contained therein will have as midcouples the decree of adjudication and the debtor's uncompleted title. Thus in the case mentioned above, where the debtor holds the property on a docket, the midcouples will be (a) the decree of adjudication, (b) the docket and (c) the confirmation of the executor who granted the docket. Where the property is held on the Land Register the foregoing remarks must be read as qualified by s 3(6) of the Act of 1979. See generally *Watson v Wilson*[3] (1868).

Subjects adjudgeable

Subject to one qualification, all heritable property is adjudgeable. Thus it is possible to adjudge not only dominium utile (though of course this is the usual case) but also superiorities, leases and heritable securities (where the adjudger is creditor of the heritable creditor). In this latter case it must be borne in mind that while heritable securities are moveable for certain purposes of succession (s 117 of the 1868 Act) they are heritable for other purposes. In addition even personal rights to heritage can be adjudged, for such rights are themselves heritable.

Adjudication is also available in certain rare cases against moveable property. This applies only where such property cannot, for technical reasons, be poinded or arrested.

The exception is where the right in question is non-transferable. The only example of this which occurs in practice is the case of a non-assignable lease. Such a lease cannot be adjudged by the creditors of the lessee. It is for this reason that inhibition does not affect such properties, for inhibition affects only such property as is adjudgeable. (See further chapter 4.)

Are missives adjudgeable by a creditor of the purchaser? Normally, though not invariably, missives are assignable by the purchaser, so it would be natural to suppose that they are adjudgeable. But in *Leeds*

3 (1868) 6 M 258.

Permanent Building Society v Aitken Malone and Mackay[4] (1986) it was held that the right of a purchaser under missives is moveable. Though there are certain exceptional cases where moveable property is subject to the diligence of adjudication, it would appear that this case implies that the only proper diligence by a creditor of the purchaser is arrestment and furthcoming. Reference is made to chapter 4 where it is suggested that the decision may be mistaken.

Common property

Though the only authority (Stewart p 584) is rather indirect, it is thought that it is competent to adjudge the share of a co-owner of heritage. It is, however, not quite clear what procedure is to be adopted once the adjudger has completed title in the Sasine or Land Register. It would seem that he cannot put in a tenant against the wishes of the other co-owner. And it is difficult to see how it would be competent to raise an action of division and sale. (See however Bell, 1,62.) It may therefore be that the adjudger can do little until he has obtained declarator of expiry of the legal. Of course, if the property is sold by the agreement of the co-owners, or by decree of the court on the application of one of the co-owners, the adjudger will be paid from the proceeds according to his ranking in relation to the share he has adjudged.

The most usual type of common property is matrimonial property, for which see below.

Matrimonial property

Title to the matrimonial home may be in one spouse, or both. Each will be dealt with in turn.

Where title is in one spouse, it is clear that a creditor of the other spouse has no claim. Occupancy rights are obviously non-adjudgeable. But the creditor of the entitled spouse is free to adjudge, and may then remove both spouses and put in a lessee. Such, at least, is the writer's understanding of the provisions of the Matrimonial Homes (Family Protection) (Scotland) Act 1981. That Act protects the non-entitled spouse from adjudications by creditors of the entitled spouse only where such adjudications are effected by collusion with the entitled spouse: see s 12 of the Act.

Where title is in both spouses, it appears that the creditors of either spouse are free to adjudge the share of that spouse who is their debtor, provided that the proceedings are not collusive: see s 12 of the Act. Once

4 1986 SLT 338.

the adjudication has been carried through, there will be enforcement problems, as discussed above in relation to common property in general.

It remains to be added that whereas protection of the matrimonial home exists in the context of sequestration (see s 40 of the 1985) Act such protection does not exist against adjudication. (Though adjudication after sequestration is incompetent under s 37(8) of the 1985 Act.)

Rights of adjudger

The adjudger cannot sell the property during the legal, though he can sell his adjudication, just as any heritable creditor can assign his security. If the debtor is in natural possession the adjudger can remove him, by court action, and then lease the property, taking the rents. If the property is already leased, the adjudger is entitled to be paid the rents. But for this to happen it is necessary for him to raise another action, namely an action of maills and duties. If the property is subject to occupancy rights under the Matrimonial Homes (Family Protection) (Scotland) Act 1981, the adjudger takes free from such rights, save in the highly improbable circumstances provided for in s 12 of that Act.

Expiry of the legal

If an adjudication has been in existence for a period of ten years (known as the 'legal'), and the debt has not been repaid (whether voluntarily, or by the rents, or otherwise), then the adjudger is entitled to convert his adjudication into a right of absolute property. He does this by an action of declarator of expiry of the legal, a Court of Session process. Such actions are rare in practice. Although the property consequences are clear—the adjudger becomes owner—it is less clear what the effect is on the debt itself. If the value of the subjects is less than the outstanding debt, is the balance still due? If the property is worth more than the outstanding debt, is the debtor entitled to call on the adjudger to account to him for the surplus? Obvious though these questions are, the writer is not aware of any authoritative answer to them. There is some discussion in Stewart at p 660.

If the subjects are held on the Sasine Register, the law appears to be that it is not necessary to register the decree. If this is the law, it is clearly unsatisfactory. An adjudger should nonetheless always take this step, for obvious reasons. If the subjects are held on the Land Register, it will be necessary to present the decree to the Keeper so that the Title Sheet may be altered accordingly.

For stamping of the decree, see above.

If the adjudger does not proceed to declarator, the adjudication remains redeemable by the debtor, as if the legal had not expired. (*Campbell v Scotland*[5] (1794).) But eventually the adjudger's title will be converted to a title of absolute property by the running of prescription. The subject is one of great complexity, and is examined in detail by the writer in an article at 1983 JR 177. It appears that the infeftment on an adjudication gives the adjudger a double title. The first is a heritable security, which takes effect at once. The other is a title of property, whose operation is suspended, and only takes effect if there is declarator of expiry of the legal. It is this latter title which is capable of being fortified by prescription.

Sale by third party

In practice the adjudger seldom has to wait ten years. Usually the adjudged property is already subject to a standard security. If the debtor is in such circumstances that he has allowed an adjudication, he will probably also have defaulted to the standard security holder. The latter, unlike the adjudger, has power of almost immediate sale. Upon such sale the adjudger will be paid any surplus since he is in the position of a heritable creditor secundo loco. (This is currently regulated by s 27 of the Act of 1970.) Even where this does not happen it is likely that the debtor will be sequestrated or liquidated long before the expiry of the ten year period. In that case the trustee or liquidator will rank the adjudger as the holder of a heritable security over the subjects, and pay him accordingly. However, there is a danger here, for the adjudger may lose his preference if his adjudication is less than a year and a day before the bankruptcy. (See below.)

Ranking

Like most other diligences, and like other heritable securities, the basic rule is that adjudications rank by date order. The relevant date is of course the date of infeftment. Thus if there is first a standard security, and then an adjudication, and then another standard security, the three rights will rank in that order. Likewise two adjudications will rank by date order. This rule is subject to a statutory exception. The Diligence Act 1661 (c 62) provides that if there is more than one adjudication, then all adjudications within a year and a day of the first shall rank pari passu with it and with each other. The details of this are complex and, it must be said, somewhat absurd. The first adjudication is defined as the one on which infeftment is first taken. But once the first adjudication has been identified, the year and day does not run from that date, but from the date of the decree on which that infeftment proceeded. Further, the adjudications which benefit from the Act are identified by date of decree not by date of infeftment, but nevertheless only qualify if the decree has subsequently been perfected either by infeftment or by registration in the Personal Register. (See *Edmonston v Thomson*[6] (1726).) The Act creates only a single equalisation period. Thus a third adjudication a year and two days after the first not only is not equalised with the first but is not equalised with the second either, even though it is within year and day of the second. It simply ranks ultimo loco.

The adjudger is the holder of a judicial heritable security on which he is infeft, and so his right will be effectual in the sequestration or liquidation of the debtor. The trustee or liquidator will pay him, as a secured creditor, according to his lawful ranking. But this general principle is subject to an important limitation, which arises from the Act of 1661 mentioned above. Every sequestration and liquidation is a deemed adjudication in favour of the trustee or liquidator on behalf of the general body of creditors. (See s 31 of the 1985 Act and s 185 of the 1986 Act. Consequently if the adjudication is less than a year and a day before the bankruptcy, it will be invalidated. (The principle here is similar to the principle operating in the case of arrestments in the sort of situation which arose in *Stewart v Jarvie*[7] (1938).) But in this connection it must be remembered that the 1661 Act only benefits those who have procured themselves infeft on their decree, or registered it in the Personal Register. Consequently in this sort of situation the trustee or liquidator should complete title as soon as possible. (See further two articles by the writer at (1984) 29 JLSS 357 and (1985) 30 JLSS 109.)

Receivership

The attachment of a floating charge is subject to the 'effectually executed diligence' of other creditor on the property of the debtor company. (See chapter 11.) The meaning of this provision has been one of the most controversial issues in the interpretation of the law of floating charges. (See eg an article by the writer at 1984 SLT (News) 177 and the references therein.) The courts have construed this provision in a minimalist way, but nevertheless there can be little doubt that an adjudication prior to the attachment of the charge will prevail against

6 (1726) Mor 13572.
7 1938 SC 309.

the charge, assuming that the adjudger has completed title on his decree. If he has decree, but has not completed title, the position is less clear. Probably in that case the charge would prevail. A particularly difficult case would be where there are two adjudications, both completed by infeftment, the second being within year and day of the first, and between the two there is the attachment of a charge. The problem here is that the first adjudication prevails over the charge, the charge prevails over the second adjudication, but the second adjudication is equalised with the first under the Act 1661 c 62. It is submitted that this situation falls to be dealt with under the ranking rules set forth by Bell at 2,405. Those rules regulate the position where the intermediate right is a voluntary heritable security, but there can be little doubt that they would apply also to the situation under consideration.

Discharge

If and when the debt is fully paid, the adjudication is discharged. Since the fee remains with the debtor, no reconveyance is necessary. But the adjudger (like a standard security holder) is under an obligation to grant (at the debtor's expense) a discharge which can be registered. If he fails to do so the debtor may and should raise an action of declarator of redemption, and register the extract decree. The expense of such an action (though not the expense of the registration) then goes against the adjudger.

Adjudication on the dependence

There is no such thing as adjudication on the dependence of an action. But a creditor who holds a liquid document of debt can, as was noted above, adjudge without constituting the debt. In addition if he holds a document of debt which is not yet liquid (eg a bill of exchange which has not yet matured) he may be able to adjudge in security. (See below.) Lastly, as already mentioned, a creditor whose debtor is in default may raise an action of constitution and adjudication even though he holds no document of debt.

Adjudication in security

Adjudication may be led on a document of debt which is not yet liquid. The creditor will of course have to aver special circumstances, since this is an extra-ordinary measure, seeing that the debtor is not yet in default. The special circumstances have in practice always been that the debtor is vergens ad inopiam. Doubtless however the same rules as to what counts as special circumstances will apply here as apply in the case of inhibitions in security. See chapter 2 above.

Adjudication in security differs from ordinary adjudication in that there is no legal. In other words the subjects remain perpetually redeemable by the debtor. But of course this difference is more theoretical than practical since, as noted above, the subjects will usually be sold by a third party such as a standard security holder or a liquidator long before the ten years have elapsed. In such a case an adjudger in security would simply be paid according to his ranking, assuming that his debt had matured. The position is less clear if his debt has not matured.

In other respects adjudications in security are subject to the general law of adjudication.

Adjudication in implement

This type of diligence is quite separate from the ordinary type. It is not a diligence for debt at all. It is an action available to a purchaser who finds that the seller refuses or fails to grant him a disposition (or other deed, depending on the circumstances of the case). The usual practice in such cases is either to resile and seek damages or to raise an action of implement. If the defender refuses to obey the order, the Court of Session may grant warrant to the Clerk to execute and deliver the deed in place of the seller. Adjudication in implement is an alternative process which is similar in effect to the implementary action just described. It is, however, more direct in that the decree itself operates as a conveyance. The procedure is to extract the decree, stamp it as necessary, and register it in the Sasine Register (with the usual warrant) or Land Register.

Adjudications in implements are not subject to the general law of adjudication. Obviously, they have no legal, and are not subject to the Act 1661 c 62.

Declaratory adjudication

Declaratory adjudication is again quite separate from adjudication in the usual sense. It is not a diligence for debt. It is available where title to heritable subjects has got 'lost' in such a way that even a resourceful conveyancer cannot transfer it to the person entitled. It is thus very much a process of last recourse. In traditional practice the most common case was where a trust had lapsed. Though still competent in such a case, it is no longer used, since remedies are available under the Trusts (Scotland) Acts.

Declaratory adjudication, like implementary adjudication, is not subject to the ordinary law of adjudication. Completion of title is the same as for implementary adjudication.

CHAPTER 14

Styles

Scope of chapter

A chapter on styles could be expanded almost indefinitely. I have
endeavoured to be brief, consistent with giving such styles as may be
required in common practice. Further styles may be had from the Scots
Style Book (1902) and the Encyclopaedia of Scottish Legal Styles
(1935).

Bill for letters: Sheriff Court Decree

The bill is prepared by the law agents for the creditor. Counsel need not
be employed.

> My Lords of Council and Session—Unto your Lordships humbly
> showeth your servitors Thalmann Freres PLC a company incorpor-
> ated under the Companies Act having its registered office at 7 St
> Matthew Square St Andrews Complainers that an action in the
> Sheriff Court of Tayside Central and Fife at Cupar at their
> instance against Zykkzyn Limited a company incorporated under
> the Companies Act 1985 having its registered office at 1 Golden
> Square Cupar Fife the Complainers on 10 November 1986
> obtained decree in their favour against the said Zykkzyn Limited
> for payment to the Complainers of the sum of FIFTEEN THOUSAND
> POUNDS with interest thereon at the rate of eleven per centum per
> annum from 29 May 1986 till payment together with THREE
> HUNDRED POUNDS of expenses all of which remains unpaid all as the
> said extract decree shown to your Lordships will testify: Herefore
> the Complainers beseech your Lordships for Letters of Inhibition at
> their instance in the premises in common form.

> According to Justice

> 'Robert Richardson'

> Robert Richardson's Bill

This style includes a signature, but this is not essential. Richardson
need no longer be a Writer to the Signet but he must be a law agent

qualified to practice before the Court of Session. Alternatively of course the Complainer may ingive the bill personally.

When the bill is passed the Clerk will write on it:

> Edinburgh 17 December 1986. *Fiat ut petitur* because the Lords have seen the extract decree. 'John Parker' Assistant Clerk of Session.

The style given here can easily be adapted to similar cases, such as a decree of the Court of Session, or other cases as given below. The exact form of the fiat may vary from case to case. If the bill has gone before the Lord Ordinary, he will sign the fiat.

Bill for letters: registered bond

This is essentially the same as above, but the narrative will differ.

> ... that Zykkzyn Limited [design as above] by their personal bond dated the 25 day of January 1986 bound themselves to pay to the Complainers the sum of FIFTEEN THOUSAND POUNDS upon the 29th day of May 1986 with interest as therein stated all as the said bond itself more fully bears, the whole of which sum remains unpaid, which said bond was registered for execution in your Lordship's Books on 1 June 1986, as an extract of said bond shown to your Lordships will testify ...

Bill for letters: depending Sheriff Court Action

Again this is similar, except for the narrative.

> ... that the Complainers have brought an action in the Sheriff Court of Tayside Central and Fife at Cupar against Zykkzyn Limited [design as above] the initial writ in which action was warranted on 4 October 1986 and served on 6 October 1986 in which action the Complainers crave the Court to decern against the defenders the said Zykkzyn Limited to pay to them the sum of FIFTEEN THOUSAND POUNDS with interest thereon at eleven per centum per annum from the date of citation till payment together with the expenses of the action all as a copy of said initial writ with deliverance and execution thereon certified by the Sheriff Clerk shown to your Lordships will testify ...

This style can be adapted to the case of a depending Court of Session action, though in practice in such a case the inhibition will be sought as part of the summons.

Bill for letters: inhibition in security

The narrative will run thus:

> . . . that the Complainers are the payees and holders of a promissory note by Zykkzyn Limited [design as above] in the sum of FIFTEEN THOUSAND POUNDS dated 1 March 1986 and payable 1 September 1986, that though the term of payment of said notes has not yet arrived the Complainers have cause to believe that the said Zykkzyn Limited are vergens ad inopiam, as which promissory notes shown to your Lordships will testify . . .

Letters of inhibition

Like the bill, the letters are prepared by the creditor's agents. Counsel need not be employed.

> Elizabeth the Second by the Grace of God of the United Kingdom of Great Britain and Northern Ireland and of her other Realms and Territories Queen, Head of the Commonwealth, Defender of the Faith, to messengers-at-arms and others our sheriffs greeting: WHEREAS it is humbly shown to us by our lovites Thalmann Freres PLC [design as above] that the complainers . . . [here give narrative, on the basis of the narrative in the bill] . . . Our will is herefore and we charge you that ye lawfully inhibit that said Zykkzyn Limited at their said registered office from selling disponing conveying burdening or otherwise affecting their lands or heritages to the prejudice of the complainer; and that ye cause register these our letters and execution hereof in the Register of Inhibitions and Adjudications at Edinburgh for publication to our lieges. Given under our signet at Edinburgh this 30th day of January in the year 1987.

Summons

The usual form of obtaining inhibition on the dependence of a Court of Session action is by including the application in the summons. This simply runs:

> This summons is warrant for inhibition on the dependence.

The signeting of the summons will then give this the force of signeted letters of inhibition.

Motion

In such cases as it is necessary to seek warrant to inhibit by a motion in a depending cause in the Court of Session, the motion is simply 'for warrant for inhibition on the dependence'.

Counterclaim

Where it is wished to inhibit on the dependence of a counterclaim in the Court of Session this is done by adding to the conclusions of the counterclaim the words 'warrant to inhibit on the dependence applied for'.

Schedule of inhibition

The writ actually served on the debtor is the schedule.

> I WILLIAM CORBETT MILLER messenger-at-arms 62 Campbell Crescent Cupar Fife by virtue of letters of inhibition signeted at Edinburgh the eighteenth day of March nineteen hundred and eighty seven years raised at the instance of THALMANN FRERES PLC a company incorporated under the Companies Acts having its registered office at 7 St Matthew Square St Andrews COMPLAINERS against ZYKKZYN LIMITED a company incorporated under the Companies Acts and having its registered office at 1 Golden Square Cupar Fife DEFENDERS in Her Majesty's name and authority lawfully inhibit you the said ZYKKZYN LIMITED defenders from selling disponing conveying burdening or otherwise affecting your lands or heritages to the prejudice of the Complainers, conform to said letters in all points. This I do upon the twentieth day of March nineteen hundred and eighty seven before and in the presence of William Glen indweller in Cupar Fife witness to the premises.
>
> 'William C. Miller'
> Messenger-at-arms.

It is the messenger-at-arms who frames this writ, not the law agent.

Execution of inhibition

The execution is the official report of the service.

> Upon the twentieth day of March in the year nineteen hundred and eighty seven by virtue of letters of inhibition signeted at Edinburgh on the eighteenth day of March nineteen hundred and eighty seven raised at the instance of THALMANN FRERES PLC [design as above] COMPLAINERS against ZYKKZYN LIMITED [design as above] DEFENDERS I WILLIAM CORBETT MILLER messenger-at-arms 62 Campbell Crescent Cupar Fife PASSED and in Her Majesty's name and authority lawfully INHIBITED the said Zykkzyn Limited defenders from selling disponing conveying burdening or otherwise affecting their lands or heritages to the prejudice of the complainers conform

to said letters in all points. A just copy of inhibition to effect as aforesaid I left for the said Zykkzyn Limited defenders with a servant within their offices and usual place of business at 1 Golden Square Cupar Fife and that for their use and behoof which copy of inhibition was signed by me and did bear the date hereof and did contain the date of signeting of said letters together with name and designation of William Glen indweller in Cupar Fife witness to the premises and hereto with me subscribing.

'William C. Miller'   'William Glen'
Messenger-at-arms   Witness

This execution is prepared by the messenger-at-arms and is returned to the law agent instructing him. It falls to be registered.

Notice of inhibition

Notice of inhibition is a writ of extreme simplicity.

NOTICE OF LETTERS OF INHIBITION
THALMANN FRERES PLC [design]
Complainers
against
ZYKKZYN LIMITED [design]
Defenders
Signeted at Edinburgh the 18th day of March in the year nineteen hundred and eighty seven.

'Sandra Filipepi' W.S.
80 Alexander Terrace
Edinburgh

Judicial recall

A petition for recall will run thus:

Unto the Right Honourable the Lords of Council and Session
The Petition of Zykkzyn Limited [design as above]
Humbly Showeth

1. That on 1 February 1988 Thalmann Feres PLC [design as above] brought an action in the Sheriff Court of Tayside Central and Fife at Cupar against the petitioners craving decree for payment of the sum of fifteen thousand pounds together with interest and expenses. The said Thalmann Freres PLC inhibited the petitioners on the dependence of said action by letters of inhibition signeted on 27 March 1988, which inhibition was served on the petitioners on 29 March 1988 and registered in the Register of Inhibitions and Adjudications on 2 April 1988.

2. The petitioners deny that the said sum is due to the said Thalmann Freres PLC. They are defending said action and have lodged a counterclaim in the sum of twenty-two thousand pounds. The full pleadings to date in said action are produced herewith and are respectfully referred to for their terms.

3. The petitioners are solvent and well able to meet any decree that might be pronounced against them in the said action.

4. The petitioners are property developers. If allowed to stand the inhibition will prevent them from carrying on business.

5. The petitioners offer to find caution for the sums sued for or such lesser sum as your Lordships may in the circumstances consider reasonable, the cautioners offered being Morag Danielle McPartlin and Patrick Syme both of 1 Golden Square Cupar Fife, the directors of the petitioners.

6. In the circumstances it is reasonable that the inhibition be recalled.

May it therefore please your Lordships to grant warrant for serving this petition on the said Thalmann Freres PLC and to ordain them to lodge answers hereto within seven days and upon resuming consideration hereof to recall the said inhibition to grant warrant for marking the same as discharged in the Register of Inhibitions and Adjudications and that upon production of a certified copy of the interlocutor of your Lordships; and to find the said Thalmann Freres PLC to be liable in the expenses of this petition and all other expenses necessary to have the said inhibition completely removed; and to decern, or to do further or otherwise in the premises as to your Lordships shall seem proper. According to Justice etc.

Discharge

We THALMANN FRERES PLC [design as above] hereby DISCHARGE the inhibition at our instance against ZYKKZYN LIMITED [design as above] proceeding upon letters of inhibition at our instance signeted at Edinburgh on the 17th, served on the 19th and registered in the Register of Inhibitions and Adjudications at Edinburgh the 21st all days of October in the year 1986. And we consent that a marking in the margin of the said Register shall be a sufficient extinction of said inhibition. And we warrant this discharge absolutely.

This should be executed as a formal deed. Different styles are in use, often concluding with a clause to the effect that the inhibitor has delivered the letters of inhibition to the grantee. Such a clause seems to lack purpose. The penultimate sentence of the style here given could likewise be dispensed with, since it is in any case implied by law.

The discharge may contain a narrative of the cause of granting, but this is not usual. For instance if the cause of granting is that the debt has been paid, it is usual to put the receipt and discharge into a separate document.

Formerly discharges were stamped at 50p, but discharges executed after 19 March 1985 are exempt from stamp duty.

Partial discharge

Partial discharge (ie restriction) has the effect of discharging the inhibition in relation to certain subjects while preserving its effect against others. It follows the style of an ordinary discharge with appropriate changes. Thus after the words 'hereby discharge' add 'but only in respect of the subjects hereinafter described'. After the inhibition has been fully identified, add: 'But always provided that this discharge is restricted in its effects to ALL and WHOLE . . .' here giving a conveyancing description of the subjects which are to be freed from the inhibition, remembering to give the reference number for Land Register properties.

Alternatively it may be that all the debtor's heritage is to be freed from the inhibition with just one exception. In that case after the words 'hereby discharge' add 'but under the exception hereafter specified'. After the inhibition has been described add: 'But always provided that the following subjects are excepted from the operation of this discharge, namely ALL and WHOLE . . .'.

Reduction

An action of reduction ex capite inhibitionis will be on the following lines. For brevity a full style is not given.

Instance in usual form.

Conclusion

For production and reduction of the disposition by the defenders Zykkzyn Limited to the defenders Fife Phoenix (Properties) (1988) Limited of all and whole . . . [insert conveyancing description] . . . which disposition between the said defenders was executed on 1 April 1989 and recorded in the division of the General Register of Sasines applicable to the County of Fife on 10 April 1989 and that ex capite inhibitionis by reason of the inhibition at the instance of the pursuers against the defenders Zykkzyn Limited signeted on 7 December 1988 served on 8 December 1988 and recorded in the

Register of Inhibitions and Adjudications on 10 December 1988; and for payment of the expenses of this action.

Condescendence

1. [Design parties.]
2. [Identify inhibition as in the conclusion. Narrate decree. Aver that debt is still unpaid.]
3. [Narrate disposition or other deed which has contravened the inhibition. Give conveyancing description of the subjects of the disposition, as in conclusion.]
4. [Aver that the disposition was in contravention of the inhibition and that the pursuers are therefore entitled to reduction.]

Plea in law

The disposition condescended upon being in contravention of the inhibition as condescended upon the pursuers are entitled to decree of reduction ex capite inhibitionis as concluded for.

Note that if the subjects are in the Land Register then it will be advisable to add to the conclusion, before the conclusion for expenses, the following words: 'And to grant warrant to the Keeper of the Registers of Scotland to give effect to such reduction in the Land Register of Scotland.'

Adjudication

For brevity this style of summons of adjudication is given in skeleton form.

Conclusions

For adjudication of the heritable property of the defender, that is to say All and Whole ... [here giving sufficient conveyancing description] ... from the defenders to the pursuers, and that for payment to the pursuer of the principal sum interest and expenses of process and extract contained in a decree for payment obtained in the Sheriff Court of Tayside Central and Fife at Cupar on 1 June 1987; According as the same shall extend when accumulated at the date of decree to follow hereon and of the interest of the said accumulated sum at the rate of eleven per centum per annum during the non-redemption of the said heritable property, and the expenses of the infeftment to follow on the said decree of adjudication with interest thereon at the rate of eleven per centum per annum from the date of disbursing the same during the non-redemption.

Condescendence

[Here design the parties. Narrate the decree. Aver that the debt is unpaid, with such details as may be necessary. Aver that the defenders are proprietors of the subjects described in the conclusion, with a reference to their infeftment in the Sasine or Land Register.]

Plea in law

The defenders having failed to obtemper the decree against them as condescended on decree of adjudication should be pronounced.

Note that when the decree is made out it ends with a 'state of accumulated sum'. This part is countersigned by the law agent for the pursuers. It will state the principal sum, the expenses, and the judicial interest, and will bring out a final figure. The interest is stated on the basis of years and days, eg 'one year and two hundred days'. Any sums recovered by the pursuers will also be entered in as deductions.

Notice of litigiosity

There is more than one type of notice of litigiosity. This style is a notice on the dependence of an action of adjudication, commonly called a notice of summons of adjudication.

NOTICE OF SUMMONS OF ADJUDICATION
THALMANN FRERES PLC (design)
against
ZYKKZYN LIMITED (design)
Signetted at Edinburgh on the twenty-fifth day of October in the year nineteen hundred and eighty seven
The summons relates to ... [here give a conveyancing description of the subjects, including the title sheet number in the case of subjects on the Land Register.]

'Sandra Filipepi'
Sandra Filipepi, Writer to the signet
80 Alexander Terrace, Edinburgh

Discharge of adjudication

We THALMANN FRERES PLC [design] considering that all sums secured by the adjudication after mentioned have now been paid to us hereby DISCHARGE the adjudication in our favour against ZYKK-ZYN LIMITED [design] by the Lords of Council and Session dated the twenty-third day of April in the year nineteen hundred and eighty eight whereon we were infeft by virtue of the recording of extract of said decree in the division of the General Register of Sasines applicable to the County of Fife on the eighteenth day of May in the year last mentioned. In witness whereof . . .

This is a very simple form. It is not necessary to give a conveyancing description of the subjects for properties in the Sasine Register, but this should be done for properties in the Land Register. The form given includes only an acknowledgement of payment and a discharge of the adjudication. This is usually sufficient but in practice the law agents for the ex-debtor will often wish to add further clauses whereby the ex-creditor formally discharges the debt on which the adjudication proceeded.

The style given covers the usual case where the adjudication does not divest the debtor, but merely gives the creditor a subsidiary real right in the subjects, namely an infeftment in security. In the much rarer case where the adjudication gives the creditor a redeemable infeftment in fee instead of an infeftment in security the discharge has to take the form of a reconveyance. In that case it is simply a disposition in common form, with an appropriate narrative, reciting the decree of adjudication, the completion of title by the adjudger, and the repayment of the debt. Fact and deed warrandice is granted.

Index

Recall —*continued*
petition, by, 31–32
recording, 33–34
restriction in case of, 29
third party, 37
Receiver
adjudication, 166–167
company law, 127–129
conveyancing practice, 147–148
party, as, 60
Recovery. *See* ENFORCEMENT
Reduction
dependence only, where inhibition
is on, 96
effect of, 94
entry in Land Register, 95
function of, 95
generally, 93
on its own, 96
procedure, 94
style,
conclusion, 175–176
condescendence, 176
instance, 175
plea in law, 176
when necessary, 95–96
Reform
proposals for, 5–6
**Register of Inhibitions and Adju-
dications.** *See* PERSONAL REGIS-
TER
Registered bond
style, 170
Restriction
discharge, in case of, 29
forms, 29
recall, in case of, 29

Sale
heritable creditor, by, 116
proceeds of, 118–119
third party, by, 165
Schedule
style, 172
Scope of chapters
bankruptcy, 117
company law, 125
creation, 7

Scope of chapters —*continued*
effect, 68
generally, 1
heritable securities, 104
parties, 57
property, 49
ranking, 78
styles, 169
Search. *See* CONVEYANCING
PRACTICE
Security
adjudication in, 167–168
bill for letters, 171
heritable. *See* HERITABLE SECURITY
inhibition as, for ranking purposes,
81–83
standard, 145–146
Security, inhibition in
consistorial causes, arising in connection with, 12
contingent debts, 10–13
creation, 10–13
debtor,
about to decamp, 11
verging on insolvency, 11
future debts, 10–13
meaning, 10
policing, 12–13
special circumstances, 11–13
Sequestration
conveyancing practice, 146
enforcement, 98
inhibition within 60 days of,
119–123
ranking, 83–85
trustee in,
party, as, 60–61
title of, 117–118
Service
debtor, on, 19
messenger at arms, by, 19
personal, 19
postal, 19
proof of, 19
sheriff officer, by, 19
Sheriff court
decree, 169–170
depending action, 170